ESSENTIALLY ATHENS

EDITED BY
KARI GUNTER-SEYMOUR

Spoken Word and Fine Art
in honor of
ATHENS, OHIO

ACKNOWLEDGEMENTS

Desire To Stay: Stockport Flats:
THE SYMBOLIC NATURE OF PETS

Rise Up Review, Issue 5, 2017:
TRUE STORY

Slant: A Journal of Poetry:
HANNAH AMONGST THE GRAVES

So to Speak: A Feminist Journal of Language and Art, summer 2014:
THAT TIME OF YEAR WHEN CHERRY BLOSSOMS

The Weather in Athens, Bottom Dog Press, 2001:
THE WEATHER IN ATHENS

EDITED BY: Kari Gunter-Seymour

LINE EDITOR: Kristine Williams

BOOK DESIGN: Kari Gunter-Seymour

COVER ART: (top to bottom) *Ridges Collage,* by Brytton Jarrett; *Honey For the Heart,* by Kari Gunter-Seymour; *Copper Vein,* by Michael Walker; *Panes,* by Chris Leonard

INQUIRIES:

gunterseymour@gmail.com

INTRODUCTION

PRELUDE

SPOKEN WORD

FINE ART

CONTRIBUTORS

EDITOR'S BIOGRAPHY

INTRODUCTION

For many years I kicked around an idea for a book, an anthology, a collection of place-based submissions of poetry, story, song and fine art focusing on Athens, Ohio. When I was selected to serve as Athens Poet Laureate, I saw my chance.

Pulling together this book has been an exercise of personal growth, discovery and joy. Every submission I received felt like a gift. The work is honest and steeped in all things Athens. I have included the fine art from the "Art Outside the Box" project; the extraordinary artworks selected to adorn the utility boxes throughout Athens City. Through this process I have become more connected to not only the writers and fine artists, but our exceptional Athens County community, a place my family has called home for three generations.

I have had the privilege of watching many Athens-based poets, songwriters and storytellers take the stage for the first time; to see that look of wonder on their face as the audience clapped and cheered their performance. I have shared time with students from Athens High School and sixth grade and have traveled as far as Virginia, to Kentucky, and throughout Ohio and West Virginia, all in the name of Athens Poet Laureate.

Word has spread. Athens, Ohio is a great place to experience remarkable poetry, story and song. Nationally and internationally recognized poets have traveled to Athens to perform for standing room only audiences. I assisted in developing a poetry trail that begins at the Dairy Barn Art Center and ends at the Kennedy Museum, a poem from a local poet for each stop along the trail. There are plans to extend the trail through three more phases.

Serving as Athens Poet Laureate has been a whirlwind of spontaneous to meticulously planned, gut laughter and hindsight 20/20. Writers in my car, my spare beds, at my dinner table, workshopping in my living room, emails and texts at all hours. Poets at the Dairy Barn Art Center, ARTS/West, the OU Inn, potluck gatherings, local bars, uptown on the street, along fence rows and under trees. Anywhere one can poet, story or sing, we have done so.

This service to my community is something deeply personal for me. A way of giving back in honor of all who reached out to me, to ease my journey and solidify my sense of belonging to this extraordinary place.

I am honored to present this collection dedicated to the heart and hearth of Athens County, Ohio.

Kari Gunter-Seymour
Athens Poet Laureate, February 2018-February 2020

This Place We Call Athens

In my life I've lived all over the country; I was born in the Pacific Northwest and have lived in 12 different cities, both large and small. Even though I had lived all over, I always felt like I was an expat from a place not yet discovered.

In early April of 1998 I drove to Athens, Ohio for a faculty interview at Ohio University. Prior to that, other than a layover at the Columbus airport when I was a teenager, I had never even been to Ohio. Yet, as I rounded the city on US 50, I knew immediately that this was where I was meant to be and was fortunate to move to Athens in the summer of 1998. For reasons I truly cannot explain, I knew I was finally home. Whether I was a Health Psychology faculty person at Ohio University, the doorman at Tony's Tavern in uptown Athens, an Athens City Council at-large member, or now, as Mayor, I've always felt connected to Athens in ways I had never felt before.

Athens is special in its sense of place and its sense of people. The rolling hills around our City define our landscape and our neighborhoods. They ascend and descend, overlap and layer. The Hocking River meanders gracefully around our community with water levels rising and lowering almost as if to have a seasonal tide of its own.

The City of Athens was established in 1797 and Ohio University was chartered in 1804 and is the oldest institution of higher education in the Northwest Territory. Our community has grown up together for over 215 years. Our history is marked by stories of people who came to Athens to attend Ohio University and never left. Or, people who came and left, only to return again. Our community has a "little bigness" about it--our small town feels much bigger than it is even though it is intimate and interconnected.

Our community is made of bricks. They are a part of who we are. Our history, our streets, our buildings have incredible historical significance and the bricks connect our past with our present. Visitors remember our bricks. Community members collect our bricks. The City of Athens residents embrace bricks in landscapes, decorations, jewelry, etc.

The people of Athens have a dynamic energy full of passion, ambition, and funkiness. Our community is known for its accepting attitudes, a broad array of creative and inventive ideas, a strong entrepreneurial spirit, a fierce commitment to social justice. Whether it's organizing the first Pride Parade, marches for women, sexual assault victims, racial equity, or gun violence, people in Athens show up and speak up. We celebrate our local and global diversity. We seek to share and learn about Appalachian cultures, traditions, and customs as much as cultures, traditions, and customs of the more than 115 countries from which Ohio University students and faculty come.

We have long been aware that our city is known as the kind of place that people like to be a part of and talk about. We are unusual, gorgeous and decidedly funky. People in Athens are enthusiastic, playful, whimsical, hopeful. We test our boundaries and share our stories. I couldn't think of a better place to be Mayor. Athens, I love you.

Steve Patterson,
Mayor, City of Athens

es•sen•tial•ly
/əˈsen(t)SHəlē/

: in essence – used to identify or stress the basic
or essential character or nature of a person or thing

Dinty W. Moore

PARADISE, FOUND

A decade ago, when I accepted a teaching position at Ohio University, a friend who had lived in the area for many years predicted I would fall in love with the tiny college town nestled in the Appalachian foothills. "Springtime in Athens," he promised, "will move you to tears."

I arrived in early summer, so had to wait through three seasons before the fragrant spring blossoms began showing themselves on the cherry trees and dogwoods, up and down every brick-lined street, along every tender hillside. My friend was right, of course. Athens in springtime is a bit of paradise.

And the Ohio University campus is the idyllic center. The blossoms, of course, flow generously across campus, but so does the red brick, streaming from building to building, along Park Place and South Court, onto the criss-crossed sidewalks of the College Green. I love how those sidewalks funnel hungry, thirsty, exuberant, and sure, sometimes stupidly drunk, bobcats through the gate and into the uptown shops and pubs, and will later funnel them back to their red-brick dormitories.

I love the mature oaks, elms, and mottled sycamores. Stately Cutler Hall. Athens County's only escalator. The mercurial graffiti wall. The Hocking River, long ago re-routed. The melancholy Ridges. This is a rich place, full of life and history.

Every season has its beauty: the humid, empty summer spaces, punctuated by concerts on the lawn and crowded street festivals; the brisk winds and orange leaves of autumn; and yes, even winter, when light dustings of snow frost the hills and sparkle in the morning sun.

And the people: the wide-eyed freshmen, dour professors, bikers, hikers, sunbathers, frisbee tossers. The eager young smiles of high schoolers on their first college tour. The concerned brows on the high schoolers' moms and dads. The Casa brunchers. The Donkey sippers. The Burrito chompers. Brew Week visitors. Motley musicians loading in and out of The Union. The hipsters, hippies, and voracious locavores milling around our heroic goats-are-for-cheese, paw-paws-are-for-eatin', artisanal-salsa, fresh-hot-pork-and-rhubarb-tamale-and-cheese-grit-laden farmers market.

Should I mention Halloween? Yes, I even love the Halloween party, probably because I have the sense to go home early, before the revelry gets out of hand.

Lovely, rowdy, unpredictable Athens.

A bit of paradise, found.

THAT TIME OF YEAR WHEN CHERRY BLOSSOMS

are enough of a shelter: Walking home, skirted
college girls are safe. One hill of the oldest

cemetery covered in spring beauties—earth
sending up its flair of confidence. Once a year, this
week without humidity, no mosquitoes at dusk.

Not yet: sudden storms that tip over trailers. Far
in the future: drenched backs of July. She
who's been drinking will hitch that ride with

a 3 a.m. stranger and will simply be taken
home. Introducing the violets, our fierce Greek
chorus, and magnolias belting Wagner until the first

rain! Beauty after a long thaw: this is the name
we'll answer to, not what the truck beds full of white boys
who think since they're truck beds full of white boys

in sun they can shout any word, any name, and we'll just have
to take it in. After this week, green will be what forces out
the gas-guzzling mower. I pray for my hair to turn

gray some days. I walk another road home, in case.
But for now, the tulips open fists pre-hollowed
by someone much gentler than me. Even red, they are

cradleble. We who look down can watch them let go,
one glossy finger curling in at a time, knowing soon
they'll give in, they'll drift on their own to the ground.

Grace Brophy Volker

WHY I WEAR A HAT

No matter how much product you slather on
the second you walk out the door
it's frizz 1, Smooth Infusion zip
Don't waste your money

You'd assume all the academic types
blowing hot air 24/7
would lower the humidity some
No such luck

Hot and steamy in the summer
cold & clammy in the winter
damp in the spring and fall
at least you don't need moisturizer

There is the rare midsummer afternoon
when the noonday sun sizzles that moistness
right out of the air
like scorched butter in a skillet

But that's a different poem

BLUE FLOWER
Liana Flores

Marlene L'Abbe

OUR TOWN

Nothing seems
surprising here
in our town

unless you count
the cashier at the grocery store
suddenly disrobing

tonight's fill-in model
for sketch class -

she has a neck
Modigliani
would die
for

Bonnie Proudfoot

NEW-2-YOU

I'm in the shoe section of the New-2-You thrift store
and let me tell you, it's a real Cinderella story.

Everyone wants shoes that are too small or too narrow --
designer knock-offs of high-heeled sandals are piled

next to well-worn clogs and sneakers shaped
like other people's feet. Next aisle over, a mother

fills a bag with children's toys, some glossy, some scuffed,
a horse-drawn coach missing only one wheel,

a sippy-cup with a pink fairy decal, her wand
an explosion of stars. Maybe someone will find a home

for a ragged straw broom with a forged iron handle,
this porcelain St. Christopher medal, hand painted

in Italy, or a sepia-toned wedding photo, framed in silver
with only the smallest chip in the glass.

Clerks shuffle through the aisles,
arranging clothes by color instead of by size,

while I look for the blue tags, 50% off,
but only the regulars know where those items are.

In ancient stories, we believe in these dazzling
threads of dreams, but in this place,

it is always half past midnight. And tonight,
my dancing boots will be shining,

though they may pinch a little. We can't
expect much, but sometimes, we get lucky.

Robert DeMott

THE WEATHER IN ATHENS

-for John Jones & Hollis Summers

Another sour March day, with no reprieve in sight:
hard to face it–winter in this hilly part of Ohio refuses to let go,

the weather here unchanged from last week and the week before;
grey the color of its moments in an already too-bleak year,

grey the shape of its bruise on the flesh of our eyes,
and no space in the heart untouched by its persistent me, me, me....

All things seem unfinished, all beginnings hard to discern—
the why and wherefore of this and that lost in noisy sleet hitting

the windshield horizontally, headlong, wipers useless on such glaze,
and in the ticking blades nothing offered up for the spirit today

but the sound of a few graveside voices complaining:
better face it—just more of the same crap—death's slick entourage,

dressed always in that certain slant of light, that gauzy something,
draped today anyway like dirty bunting from headstones

pitched among acres of bell-shaped narcissi whose mouths
no longer nod their secrets in our calamitous air.

CHURCH BELLS (SONG)

The church bell's gonna ring everyday right at noon
But I just can't predict everything
You said you're gonna call me some day real soon
But I just don't know when it's gonna be

You've been leading me on
You've been leading me out
Down the road, up the trees, to the sky
I've been thinking about you
You're showing up in my dreams
But I still sleep alone at night

The mail's gonna come between ten and eleven
And the door's gonna close right at five
And I'll sit in the bar and drink whiskey till seven
Just hoping that you might stop by

You've been leading me on
You've been leading me out
Down the road, up the trees, to the sky
I've been thinking about you
You're showing up in my dreams
But I still sleep alone at night

The band's gonna play on Saturday night
And if you don't show up by sundown on Sunday...

The trash man picks up every Monday
And the newspaper boy's never late
And the city bus runs every hour going both ways
So how long do you think I can wait

You've been leading me on
You've been leading me out
Down the road, up the trees, to the sky
I've been thinking about you
You're showing up in my dreams
But I still sleep alone at night

The church bell's gonna ring everyday right at noon

CASA COMMUNION

Caught still in the spell
Of the Coolville Hot Club's
Sultry jazz with its
Django Reinhardt gypsy swing,
I walk home in the dark
Over Athens' brick streets.
What matter a summer shower
Clears the air even as
Warm wetness soaks through
Down glistening streets made new
Deserted by others so long abed
The beauty of street light
Illuminated rain just for me,
The world transformed,
Made sane again by music
And holy water.

PANES
Chris Leonard

Patricia L.H. Black

TEAMWORK WORKS

On Ohio's Hocking River, somewhat to the south,
at the mid-point of the river, nowhere near the mouth,
the Athens Punt and Rowers Club struck out away from shore
to execute maneuvers that they were famous for.
The brawny Eight from Athens could row against the flood
even when the Hocking's waters were congested thick with mud.
When rowing with the current they flew as eagles fly,
soaring swift as angels 'twixt the water and the sky.
The rhythm of their rowing was a sight to warm the heart
with their metronomic coxswain excelling at his art.
His steady rhythmic calling of the stroke was fine to hear
and since only he faced forward, it was up to him to steer.
But a night of dissipation in the taverns of the town
felled the doughty coxswain; he was sorely taken down
by gout and flu and quinsy and ills too lurid here to tell—
he could scarcely raise a whisper; he surely could not yell
instructions to his rowers out on the river's face.
They had to find a substitute to take the coxswain's place.
A drummer from a jazz band volunteered to do the task
of commanding Athens' rowers; all they had to do was ask.
So they all took to the river and everything was grand;
bar a bit of acclimation, they had the scull in hand.
Up the river then they went, a dozen miles or more,
and the coxswain kept them moving, well away from shore.
They were fine until the coxswain, the cheeky little bloke,
put a touch of syncopation in his calling of the stroke.
With "Stroke! Stroke!" forsaken for "Stroke and heighdy-ho!"
One man stroked on "Heighdy", the next one stroked on "Ho."
The third man asked the fourth one, "Did you understand that call?"
Quite discombobulated, Number Five stroked not at all.
Numbers Six and Seven ducked together, as of one accord,
As the eighth man grabbed the coxswain and threw him overboard.

TWO PLACES TO LOOK FROM

1.

They come here. They become part of the fun. They become rooters for the team. They wear the colors and they march down the main street. They march holding pennants and souvenir mugs. The streets have been closed for them. The parking meters are covered with plastic bags for them. The police stand around for them in the crowd. The crowd wears the green-and-white too. The crowd cheers for them. On the bricks they march. They raise a cheer, and another cheer, and another cheer. They seem to be at One.

2.

They are awaiting arrest. They are letting the media know here is news and a protest worthy of news. They are protesters on the paved brick intersection at Court and Union. Holding signs and holding things up, so that people pay attention to the injustice they wish to expose.

People pass who may be opposed to their thinking. Who may not even have on their radar what they want them to think about. No one gets hurt here. There are no bats or guns in holsters. They sit there, some with children in their laps, waiting to be arrested. A dozen or so agreed to be arrested.

Others back away onto the street corners. When the light changes the mass of protestors, and anyone along coincidentally, cross from corner to corner along the quad (there may be a hundred now), prevented from using the diagonal X-crosswalks by the police.

Cross and cross and cross. Cheers and songs and defiance of the injustice other people may find not worth bothering about, perhaps. Perhaps not. Some only on their way to class may wish they could be arrested too. Some on their way to jobs after lunch may wish they could be arrested too.

With their drums on the bricks, baby blankets on the bricks, jeans, suits, poster board signs, seriousness of purpose on the bricks.

Wendy McVicker

ON POETRY PATROL AT THE CANTINA

Behind me, they are laughing
and talking about a book,
or a film, they have seen.
His voice is languid, slow,
the voice of a late riser,
still warm and furry
with sleep, rumpled sheets
twisted at the foot
of his words.
Her voice jumps
and dances, her sentences
pounce, tease, burrow
into his pauses.
Plates clink, water
shivers in my glass,
and when they get up
to leave, he brushes
his long slow fingers down
her shoulder, her dreadlock
coiling its open
question, and she flicks
that honeyed tongue under
his chin, and they laugh,
and it's spring outside,
redbuds slipping
magenta beads along
their silver limbs,
and they laugh, parting
the shadows between
our tables, and vanish
into the light.

ATHENS COUNTY LINE (SONG)

Fog is laying on the trees
Sun is swinging low
Took my time a-getting here
Headed back as fast as I can go
And I'll be feeling fine
Take a load right out my mind
Soon as I catch sight
Of that Athens County line

'Cause I'm just working toward home
Work my way on down this road
'Til I can pull into the drive,
See my baby's smile, and fold into her arms
Dog sniffing on the tires
Checking out just where I've been
They don't tell time the way we do
But I'm more like them than I'm like you
'Cause in the morning when I go
I get just ten miles off the farm
And it's already been a long, long while
And I just want to turn around
But I got ninety more to drive
And then ten hours on the job
And it wears its way real thin
But looking back on where I've been
Only Love's been on my side

(Chorus)
And I don't know why
But I'm more connected all the time
Can't stray too far
From my baby's arms

And everything is fine
Take a load right off my mind
Soon as I catch sight
Of that Athens County line

And it's just another do and die
You push the good on thru the bad
Might be another damn cliché, but one fine sunny day
I'll turn it 'round and take it home
One fine day, I'll stay

And I'm just working toward home
Work my way on down this road
'Til I can pull into the drive, see my baby's smile
And fold into her arms
Dog sniffing on the tires
Checking out just where I been
They don't tell time the way we do
But I'm more like them than I'm like you…

(Chorus)

BIRD AND MANDELA
David VanShoor

STUDIO ARTS 101

He was unconventional.

He was unconventional and waggish,
spontaneous and absurd.

He was spontaneous and absurd,
and so damn honest.

He was so damn honest, we
his students gave notice,
cast aside artifice and vogue,
shouted *hell no* to words
being the only names we went by.

He pushed us nest-less,
paint posturing, paper twisting
wildings, our fingers
stained and greasy,
orphans of outdated syllabi.

Our creations astounded us,
and we rejoiced.

We were newborn, and he
was so damn honest and absurd,

and we did so,

oh,
how we did,
so

love him.

Felix Gagliano

THE BIKE PATH IN ATHENS, OHIO

Officially it is the Hockhocking Adena Bikeway
but Athenians just call it "the bike path."
Ancient ghosts smile at both these names
for they know about earlier users of this trail.

I ponder them as my bike rolls on this blacktop ribbon,
a slender asphalt snake beside the Hocking River.
It is a rail trail, built atop a disused railroad easement,
that once bore tracks that train wheels clicked over.

Before iron horses, it was a towpath for the Hocking Canal,
where mules once pulled vessels through a water channel.
Manufactured goods glided into Athens upon this liquid road;
salt, iron, coal, wool and lumber slowly returned north upon it.

Animals probably first blazed this trail, maybe even dinosaurs.
Hockhocking Adena Indians walked here too, 2000 years ago.
My bike follows in the wake of these caravans of prior pilgrims.
Time has erased their footprints but memories of them endure.

Today wise eyes can still spot souvenirs of these past travelers:
a fossil, an arrow head, a railway spike or ruins of a canal lock.
I wonder who and what will use this way worn path tomorrow?
What faint remnants will they find of now and us (and me)?

AT THE PRESCHOOL WHERE
I WORK PART-TIME AS A SUB

You say that Lacie is broken
as I hold the sweaty three-year-old
rocking her like an infant. My biceps
burn and my back aches and I have
stripped off my sweater even though
it is January and so cold the snow
squeaked as I walked to my car
in the dark this morning, resenting,
just a little, that I am parked
in the driveway because there
are now two cars that you are
fixing in the twin bays, one
with the engine hanging over it
for the last five years, the little
Subaru WR-X with the turbo that
I drove much too fast, young
mother, always rushing from
one place to the next with home
far down on the list of places
I must be right now. I rushed
to meet the bus and to work and
rushed my children:
go, hurry up, foot tapping.

I am not rushing now. Lacie,
body heavy, sags against me.
I try to ease her down onto a cot
one   move   at   a   time
because she fights sleep like it is
a dragon. And maybe it is, given that she
and her sister have grown up
in Athens County, Ohio, poor and girls.
I watch how she plays peek-a-boo
with her baby sister like the woman she
someday might be, how she eats food

from under the tables, maybe
the only way she gets enough to eat
at home and
my heart rips.

I cannot put her back together,
can't even put myself back
together now that I have retired and
lost who I always thought I was. But I
can hold Lacie, swaying back and forth,
can drape my sweater over her so the
light reflecting off of the snow outside the
window doesn't wake her just yet.

Teagan Hughes (class of 2019 at Athens High School)

BROKEN DOWN

i am from the self-contained unit.
broken, yet healing
yet constantly changing.
i am made of the instinct to run;
the natural impulse to get three hours away from here
in a rusted-out Oldsmobile.
my people are from wherever they could get by;
from rows of worn and shuttered houses
from where,
if you were being buried alive,
you were handed a shovel
and told to
dig yourself out.

HANNAH AMONGST THE GRAVES

(for Charles Kerns 8.9.1944 #931)

Hannah is a picture amongst the graves,
her long hair whipping about in a wonder
of dark curls, spring rain unpredictable as madness.
She scans the rows of headstones, searching
for her great grandfather who retains his past,
his name, among the nameless dead of the asylum.

Two-thousand dead at the Athens Asylum
for the Insane, and their numbered graves
tip and slide into corrosion, sink into the past.
19, 84, 930: few remember, or visit, or wonder –
each number a page in the landscape's story, searching
for its reader, its interpreter of madness.

And what of madness?
Hannah seeks the secrets of the asylum:
intemperance could have set his loved ones searching
for assistance; or perhaps he was just mean and grave
or rakish, as her family has often wondered –
they were too young when he died to recall his past.

But from the dark eyes of the attic windows, the past
looms, spreading shadows that can drive one to madness.
How can she not think of him, how can she not wonder
about those days before Thorazine, the horrors of the asylum,
electric shock and lobotomies sending men to early graves
while the locals lunched on the hospital grounds, searching

for stones to skim across blue lakes. This search
for meaning haunts her family for generations past,
so they take up a collection, add his name to the grave-
but this, they know, is no cure for madness.
Does his ghost remain tethered to the asylum –
just one of many reported to roam in wonderment

at their own losses? Do they watch in silent wonder
at our modern advances? How Hannah finds herself, searching
for hereditary secrets etched in the records of the asylum:
For a glimpse of her future, she unearths her past,
whether she find love, or pain, or madness.
So hard to stifle that chill at these graves

as she wonders if the madness will strike her.
She searches the past: is there a warning in the DNA
engraved on the tomb of her heart – or asylum?

STUDENT NURSES AT THE LUNATIC ASYLUM

Crowning the thousand-acre campus like a gowned and jeweled Victorian queen,
The lavish administration building displayed cut flowers, polished wood, and whispers.
Freud, food, and fresh air…the only good treatments available at the time.
But…there were many bad ones, some neglect, and a bit of exploitation.

Green folds of the vast estate cradled three cemeteries, the remains of almost 2,000.
Large scattered brick buildings held the living, committed for care, away from society.
Inside these buildings, fear had its own recognizable scent. Furtive whispers were heard,
whimpering and crying, screams and lamentations.

Many moved freely about the estate, tending to the gardens, cleaning, working
the power plant.
But Ruby never left her building. She never uttered a sound as she worked the hallways.
First, she'd affix a heavy mop head using some unwritten set of directions,
Always ending in the same sharp click. She never looked up, but knew precisely
where she was.

Each elbow rose exactly to the correct level and every inch of ten square feet of floor was
covered. Then, dunk, wring, shake, and begin again for another ten square feet.
Her medical record revealed that she used to look up, but her husband, her children,
her mother…they never came. "Study her chart, Try to engage her." Those were our orders,
but how to do it…no one seemed to know.

The lights were always dim in Annabelle's room, a room of silent children. Her crib
was too small. She'd soon need another, if she lived. Her head outgrew her little body,
puffed around her face. Her baby mouth, her pretty blue eyes. Carefully, we cleaned
and turned her, tried to protect her neck, tried not to make her cry. But we cried.

When Manford returned to his building, he had been in the hospital ward for months.
His chart revealed that he had not been expected to survive. It was all his own fault,
and now he was locked up. But did he know it? Did he hear us when we talked to him
softly? Was he in there? Manford put his head into the circular saw at the wood shop.
He must have given up.

Louie must have thought he'd come upon the perfect gift as he excavated the loamy soil
to retrieve it. How he had remembered the place, he didn't know. They had cut his brain.
The past, the present…

So like a movie. Louie carefully cleaned the prize and wrapped it in his shirt. It was lovely,
smooth and round. The perfect gift for his favorite nurse.

MAGIC MOUNTAINS
Michael McDowell

HOMETOWN

I was asked about growing up here and I didn't know where to start.
I hate this town.
I hate this tiny speck of "civilization."
I hate our river–pardon me–our creek.
I hate that we're always unprepared for any amount of snow.
It reeks of hometown, of simple life, of loud family.
The stench of staying clings on everyone who passes through.
It smells of seventh generation, of "born-and-raised,"
of "buried-by-the-cornfield."
I hate watching my friends come and leave, transient and temporary.
I hate the changing culture, the new additions, the "up-and-coming."
I hate being the last of my class, of a generation past;
a man who stayed too long.

Little memories, the too-common barbs, cling and cloud
my subconscious.
Of every time the power went out and we had to eat by candlelight.
Of the same old boring pizza every Friday night.
Memories of tiny, cheap, fireworks reflected in the waters.
Of the peepers screaming by my window late into the night.
Of chasing fireflies into tick-riddled tall grasses.
Memories of exploring the empty woods behind my house.
Of the muskrats and cicadas and mystery cocoons.
Of friendships forced by a cul-de-sac surrounded by miles of nothing.

Memories of sleeping through my graduation
and sobbing at my baptism, of the nights-too-late
with friends and the mornings-too-early in worship
and the quiet, perpetually-uphill walks well past
midnight, of the throbbing-music parties on Court
and the heated debates about our four dollar
movies and the deep talks under the stars and the
slow kisses by fires and the quiet rains and the
quieter snows and the half million sunrises and
the fishing on the docks and the, and the...

I hate this town.
I hate how much I'll hate to leave.

Melanie Moynan-Smith

YOU CAN'T MAKE ME HATE

You can't take away my smile
And fill me full of hate
You can't divide me from my neighbor
Or my country or my state

You can't rob me of religion
And wish my beliefs would die
You can't kill me with your guns
And think it's justified

Violence isn't righteous
Bigots say no more
Weapons aren't the answer
I don't want your racist war

I'm not listening to your hate speech
I'm not repeating all your labels
Your language is offensive
To many, many people

Hate is not the answer, tolerance and love prevail!
I respect my neighbor, and peace be in our land
There is no room for violence and destruction
Towards Mother Earth and man.

Devin Aeh

LIGHT POLLUTION

there are questions I don't ask
mostly
do you remember
do you regret
is it everything you wanted

i'm still in the country, with my dogs
staring up at the sky knowing i'm not god
neither is money
nor other people's opinions of me

i bet you can't even see the stars
from where you are

Pamela Kircher

WEST UNION STREET CEMETERY

Have you noticed
that this being alive
is a strange thing?

Sometimes no different
than the rhythmic ringing of chimes
filling up night
then dying away.

It's a little like breath,
isn't it? And sometimes
things that scare us
stop scaring us and call
come closer

Across the street
the black chain swoops from post to post
along the graveyard road.

A rope to follow
past grave stones
cloaked in vagrant street light
to separate themselves from the night.

Not so the iron dog
split at the seams, the inner dark
releasing homeward to night.

It's never empty, the iron dog
perfect in its purpose:
to be there
like sorrow,

long after the moon has washed the streets
and left them drifting
in other people's forgetful sleep.

UNTITLED
Karen Renee

Sean Kelbley

TRUE STORY

All the way home on Tuesday
I listened to the news about coal,
how yes it would/no it wouldn't

Put People Back to Work, Increase
Energy Independence, Kill the Planet.
And Tuesday night, no lie, for the first time

I can remember, every car of the train
that passes in our valley was a coal car,
every car mounded full of coal,

as if somewhere across the Ohio River
a horde had been seething on stand-by God
knows how long, just waiting for pen-stroke

permission to fill up trains with mountaintops
and shove them north. It happened that fast,
the news and then the train, and it's true:

I didn't fully believe what I was seeing
even as I saw it, and felt—still feel—
how someone must when a UFO

flashes across the sky above their deck, or Bigfoot
lumbers through their high beams as they drive
a lonely township road, or some other thing

some say has never been, shouldn't ever be,
suddenly is, and there's no one to ask

Did you see those lights? What's that
running into the woods?

BLUE IRIS
-after Mary Oliver

What about the blue iris?
The bleeding heart?

Tall Ironweed's red stalks
and purple starbursts

brightening your desk,
the morning field?

Do you see how
attention is the beginning of devotion?

The damselfly's blue,
body slim as a hat pin;

even at rest,
her green crosshatch wings

held ready for launch?
How the yellow pear on your desk

ripens?

YELLOW FORSYTHIA

I was going with the Athens Senior Group to the Washboard Company in Logan a few years ago. It was supposed to snow the next day, and I wanted it to count as one for the 3 days of snow after the yellow forsythia comes out, so we could get the snow over with.

We had already had the first day of spring and an early Easter, and I still hadn't seen any forsythia in Athens. After looking all the way up to Logan, and coming back the scenic route of New Marshfield, I said I was going to "zap" one to appear.

The ladies said maybe they froze out, but I said we would still see some traces of the elusive forsythia. Where are the blooming bushes?

I was looking out the window of the van going "zz", and I heard a haiku poem, 5-7-5 syllables in my head (I made it up). I recited it to the people emphasizing the z-sounds jokingly.

"The Forsythia"

Freezing till the zephyr breeze
Whispering of spring
As we entered Athens,
And came past Larry's
Dawg House, and went up
Past Hungry Howie's pizza on
Union Street, there was a
Gorgeous, voluptuous,
Fabulous yellow forsythia
Bush, right across from
The old Ziegler Grocery
Store! Exquisite! Sweet!
They were surprised.
I wasn't.

SQUIRRELS

Agile, furry and gray,
Oh, how they like to play.
Jumping up and down,
Running all around,
On tree branches in and out.
Gaily playing all about.

They are so quiet and cute,
But my bulbs they uproot,
To squirrels, they must be tasty
Planting new? Won't be hasty!
Every time I've planted,
Noisily they've ranted,
My garden, their cellar is,
In and out in just a wiz.
They don't care when I yell,
They just run and tell,
Tasty morsels to be had,
For me it is just too bad.

When the ground with snow is white,
Many squirrels are in plain sight.
Walnuts and bulbs now in the ground
All winter long for them to be found.
In my trees they've built their nests
Where on cold winter days they rest.
No worries, plenty food is stored,
You can tell, they are never bored.

Squirrels having so much fun,
As they climb, play and run.
Agile, furry and gray,
I hope they're here to stay.

John Thorndike

IN THE OUTHOUSE

Don't look back, the mystics say
but oft they foul their nest,
and there's a steaming pile below
that occasions this request.

Help to speed divine decay
and ease the situation,
by throwing in both lime and sawdust
with each evacuation.

Todd Bastin

MY OLD HOME

I grew up in the country on a wooded ridge
that ascended to grassy slopes
overspread with wild purple raspberries and pink bergamot
and underlain by groundhog burrows and rabbit warrens
the old-timers called it Morrison-Brown Hill
though no official road sign bears this name
the rambling apple and lush cherry trees in our yard
in their flowering beauty evoked the old homestead
a hardscrabble farm that had straddled our hilltop
but was subdivided in the sixties and sold off
to people who worked in town like my parents
here they could have homes with gardens and quiet
and let the birdsong settle into the soul
my parents' vegetable garden required no fence
because the deer preferred to forage from nature
than to bother with what my mom and dad had planted
for there was plenty of woods and wild meadow back then
sometimes cows from a neighboring farm would escape
and come climb up the steps of our concrete porch
to take a break from the sun, to rest and ruminate
stressing my parents but making me laugh
my brother was my playmate in those days
we played in and ran through green grass full of violets
the safety bases for our tag games were huge trees
with gnarled surface roots like rocky islands
motley plants and pretty weeds carpeted my imagination
a pair of swaying willows caught every mood of the wind
and a grand old silver maple had a swing
suspended from a high branch
if you dared you could go sailing into the sky

HILLS
April Felipe

Wenda Sheard

THE DEER IN MY FOREST

The deer in my forest come not from Europe,
Like my grandparents a century ago.
The deer shop not at big stores
     for goods from China and Japan,
Nor at gas stations
     for oil from Iraq and Kuwait.

The deer wander with their ancestors' purpose,
Shopping locally, without taxation,
     without for representation,
     oblivious of human history.

The deer, if they knew, would laugh
     at my claim to the forest,
A claim lying on paper,
Paper they cannot read,
Paper buried from sunshine
     in a county office
     many trees away.

Deer hearts break in November
     as mothers and brothers die,
For the fun and food of
     European descendants,

Descendants who know not foods of the forest,
     Or calm lights of dawn,
     Or gentle rains of the darkness,

Rains trying in vain
     To wash clean
     Our human sins
     That harm the home.

OUT BACK

I walk across the field tilled years ago,
half covered now with buildings and parking lots,
and let the dog go out back
where whitetail come from the woods at night
looking for scraps from past harvests.

Sunset after a day of teaching school
and the clouds spit veins of firelight
across the miles between this ridge and the next
after the kids wandered through books
and history, feeling like ghosts.

They traveled together while I watched,
waiting to see their discoveries and sunsets,
borne by creatures alive,
searching, like me, out back for answers.

MY BRICK HOUSE

I am a widow and live alone, but I am not alone. My house is very old and I often talk to it, the wood, brick and brass. I touch the tweens on every pass and whisper, "I love you." Sometimes, when I am quiet, I feel the warmth of love and something else. I feel a discomfort and swell of overwhelming sadness. The others tell me my house is haunted.

This house was built on one man's dream and holds the story of a country doctor, Peter Thomas Burns. He was born into a farming family of ten children. That land was granted to his ancestor for serving in the revolutionary war and was successfully farmed with every generation thereafter, but Peter wanted more.

He left the family farm, said goodbye to his sweetheart, Miss Martha, and ran off to medical school in Cincinnati. Upon graduation, Peter and Martha married. Together, they purchased a three acre parcel of land in Athens County on what was a piece of the original Stewart farm. They built a double brick, proper doctor's house and moved in with their two sons, Daniel and Edward. Martha soon gave birth to their third child, Howard. Two years later, a daughter, Louise, entered the family. Martha cared for the children while Peter tended to his patients making house calls in the surrounding hills or seeing them in his home office. However, there is evidence that things were not always pleasant behind closed doors in the doctor's house.

Dr. P.T. Burns was fond of the drink and sometimes experimented with certain chemical preparations locked in his office cabinet. He became a harsh, unforgiving husband and father refusing to let his children leave when they became of age. He needed to control them and it was his mission to keep the children, even as adults, dependent upon him.

In 1910 Daniel was 30 years old, farmed a portion of the property and became a master carpenter. Edward, 25 was a mailman. Howard and Louise, 23 & 21 respectively, were school teachers. The once lovely lady Martha grew tired and worn, but took care of them all. Before the decade was over, the silent secrets locked within the walls would seep out into world.

Daniel spent time as a patient in the Athens State Hospital up on the ridge and the following year, Edward mysteriously died. There is no record of how or where, only that his death occurred in 1911. Soon thereafter,

Daniel moved out of the family home against his father's wishes and settled in the town of Athens. Louise left and married a man from a prominent family in 1914, never to speak of her father or brothers again. And then there was Howard.

He was the first child to be born in my house and his mother's favorite. He was a sensitive, odd and often withdrawn child who had difficulty fitting in with the other boys. His exacting and often intoxicated father made life unbearable for Howard. Newspaper accounts state that Howard was in ill health and that is what caused his death in 1916. I know something very different happened.

On August 27, 1916, Howard was committed to the Athens State Hospital. He remained there for 10 days before he was released to his parents. Life in general and particularly life in his father's house was an unspeakable torture for Howard. So, very early the next morning, Howard took a rifle and shot himself. His father found him dead.

Howard is still here in my house. His father never wanted him to leave and being the dutiful son, he never did. He is still sensitive and withdrawn, but I don't think he's odd. I wonder if he is seeking the love and acceptance his father would not, could not give him.

Sometimes, when I talk to my house, the wood, brick and brass I touch the tweens on every pass and whisper to Howard, "I love you."

COURT STREET QUINTESSENCE

Along these bricks, with rain-washed gleam,
I move slowly through the stream
of vaguely-familiar, yet unknown faces.
Everyone hurries to drier spaces
without noticing the beauty unfurled
like a pennant in this busy world.
I can't help but drop all my defenses
and let free all my bound-up senses;
pay heed to azure inkpot painted sky
with hundreds of strangers rushing by
heedless, looking for the day's last beer,
each with unique stories that I can't quite hear.

Now that I'm aware, I can't use just eyes;
not with a host of scents that tantalize
on the wind. The ghosts of ketchup and herbal smoke
cling to air so thick and wet it chokes;
strange spices blend with the burnt brown haze
of the weary, bitter brew of the day's
last cup of coffee. I also sense
the jumbled, left behind essence
of the familiar strangers passing through, cast off –
with piercing perfume that makes me cough.

So much for scent; I turn to ears
eager to relate all that they hear.
So loud tonight, a merry tangle
of jackhammers percussing bright summery jangle
of guitars in the mild winter air. The players curse
when one of them forgets a verse;
but still I stop and listen awhile,
then put the day's last loose change in the hat with a smile
as the footsteps of fellow strangers beat bright
along these rain-gilt bricks tonight.

HONEY FOR THE HEART
Kari Gunter-Seymour

Kiki Chen (Class of 2019 at Athens High School)

HOMECOMING

ohio, not greece, not the smooth slide of marble on skin but the catch of sweaters on brick

i was born the same year as these classic georgian buildings (2002), which my professor hates because they imply slavery. sometimes, i almost believe they mean it. here, we're all a little bit liars. the greeks knew it then — everything is more precious when it's rare. even truth. especially truth.

swaddle me in cigarette smog, collegiate green sadness, and pickup truck parades, and i will thank you for taking me home. in the tightest fist of winter, it smells like smoke at the edge of the world, which is found at the end of my driveway.

did you know that 18 weekend hours spent putting on a Prom will change you on a molecular level? and did you know that when it rains very hard the Hocking river creeps onto the soccer fields next to Walmart, bringing a legion of worms? and did you know in 1970 the bushes were flooded with tear gas, and my high school geometry teacher and childhood pastor and middle school cross country coach can tell you all about it? these bricks are made of boogie and blood.

drag me through the streets by burrito buggy until the fiberglass in my chest shatters

the castle on a hill is real, but its walls aren't. i am racing the train which is rearranging my molecular structure into a blacktop on a February day. i'm sorry i took so much from you, and i'm sorry i'm going to pay it back, even the parts i shouldn't. what is life but a permanent state of missing something?

in the concentric ring of communities in which we all exist, this town is the third. not the inferno, nor a celestial space. it is purgatory, in the opposite direction. i am in love with empty hallways, and my worst fear isn't leaving. it's coming back to find that i can't remember you.

greek high schools and english streets and gas stations entirely american.
this is the kind of place where you can eat pesto baguettes in a field and think about the days of the week. i am from here and not here and the soft spot on the underside of your bicep. this is the kind of town you can't wait to get out of, and then come home to again.

Erika Williams

SO ENTER DAILY THOU MAYEST GROW IN KNOWLEDGE WISDOM AND LOVE

It would be a cliché to say
I could navigate the winding
roads to my parents' house
in my sleep but that doesn't
make it any less true. The
topography of this town is
etched straight into my heart
and guides me home from
lightyears away.

The first time I drove alone
was the evening I got my
license. I told my mother I
needed to pick up groceries.
I was gone for hours, driving
the streets of Athens--streets
I had grown up watching go by
in the side mirror.

I don't know how anyone
chooses to leave, but
somehow we do. We reach
beyond the city limits to find
bigger, bolder cities
but Athens is always there
to welcome us home. To
remind us that there are
trees and creeks and hills
that remember our names.
They remember the time
before we were here, and
they will remember after.
They remember the first time
our cat ever ran away, and
how we frantically searched,
crying her name until our

voices grew hoarse. They
remember her coming home,
shaking, muddy, and drenched
in rain. Our tears leaked into
her fur, leaving our love
permanently on her skin.
My father buried her in
the woods behind the
house two days ago–matted
fur and years of love lowered
beneath the soil, a part of our
hearts buried with her.

When I was eighteen I
moved away, but I did not
go far. I settled into college
life easily, living a mere ten
minutes away from my family.
I navigated the streets differently
than I had before, trudging
to class and stumbling upon
the bricks at night. I made
lifelong friends among
those brick roads and buildings,
and we nestled into couches
and library stalls
and twin sized beds.

When I was twenty-two,
I left for one of those
bigger cities.
I can still feel the fear in
my bones. It did not last long,
and Athens called me home.
The comfort of my mother's arms
wicked away any sadness
I felt, and my laughter came
from Friday night pool uptown
with my father.

I fell in love with Athens.
I fell in love in Athens.
I left again, recently, and I
whisper home to Athens at night.
Because no matter where
I find myself, I can always
find my way home.
The bricks and trees and buildings
and hills will be there when I am
ready to return. They,
along with my family, will
embrace me with open arms,
and remind me that
this place is unlike any other.

No matter how hard you try
to replicate Athens,
you will never fully do so.
It's still there, and it always will be,
waiting to welcome you home.

COPPER VEIN
Michael Walker

Leah Swatzel

OLD HIGHLAND PARK

Today where a modern playground lay
There's shown no sign of the good ol' days
Where every minute was never dark
And so existed Old Highland Park

And on Mondays, Fridays; any days
The kids would go, and they would play
They'd tumble down the rusty slide
And someone would seek and the others would hide

And the swings would screech when given weight
And then would wail while swinging straight
The youth believed they were singing song
And the parents told them they were wrong

And the monkey bars were friends of ours
The kids dreamt they were hanging stars
And there's that tunnel that we crawled right through
And was so unsafe it was made of glue

But now those things are gone today
And the next generation goes there to play
They don't realize what was there before
But those who remember tell tales galore.

Leah Swatzel is a 6th grader who attends Morrison-Gordon Elementary and lives with her
little brother, mom, dad, and goldfish in Athens, Ohio. Leah has always had a love for writing,
debating and school in general, and could sit down and have a conversation with anyone.

Savannah Rapp

WE ARE NOT POOR

According to the internet,
Athens is poor.
But money doesn't matter.
Not in this little town of ours.
We have all of our places,
We have all these kind people
And all the different vibes.
Almost everyone knows everyone.
And you've been everywhere
Big cities always have something new,
New things to see
And new people to meet.
But we have close friends,
We have love
And we have fun.
Visitors might say something is missing,
But nothing was ever lost.
We may not have lots of money,
But our culture is unique.
We have everything we need.
We are NOT poor.

Savannah Rapp is a 6th grader who attends West Elementary and lives with her family, three cats and a dog in Athens, Ohio. She is an Irish dancer, gardener, baker, animal lover and loves to write. Her favorite things to write are poems. She loves anything vibrant, happy and positive.

ATHENS

Rich and growing
Athens
Alive and bustling
Green grass as soft as snow
The trees rustle as if to talk
Animals race past
Under the great canopy of leaves
You are right there
Standing still
Listening
Watching,
Waiting
The birds chirp
As you listen
To their beautiful music
The city life moves around you
Loud and blaring
But you ignore it
Watching
As dusk turns to night
The town falls in shadow
And night is full,
You are still there
All through the night
Up in the morning you see
The town growing alive with life
Athens
This is my life
Athens
This is my home.

Emerson Crowl is a 6th grader at East Elementary in Athens, Ohio. He has two older
siblings and a dog, Juno. He likes to play soccer and on rainy days, he likes to delve deep
inside his favorite book at home.

GLORY ATHENS

Oh glorious Athens
Just hear our bobcats roar
You see bobcats everywhere you go
Everywhere there's history
In a state shaped like a heart.
It is home.
Here in Athens
You'll always have friends
Beautiful forests, glorious hills,
The east and the west, adventure here, fun over there,
For some it's our hearts, for some, their home,
To some it's both.
For in all of glorious Ohio, Athens is the best
For that we have, all that we love that's here,
It's still all in Athens, oh Glory Athens.

Han Keith Callerame was born on July13, 2007 in Tucson, Arizona. His family moved all over the country. His sister was born on November 13, 2009 in Aurora, Illinois. He lives currently alternately between living with his dad in Alameda, California, and living with his mom in Athens, Ohio. Han has a very strong love for technology and memes that is always growing.

Kyle Schleter

THE PLAINS / NEW YORK

The Plains
Small Quiet
Unchanging Walking Sneaking
GiGi's, The Plains Public Library, Empire State Building, Central Park
Sprawling Changing Bustling
Lively Loud
New York

Kyle Schleter is a 6th grader who goes to The Plains Elementary School in Athens, OH. He likes Harry Potter and just relaxing around his house. He also loves fennec foxes, red pandas and monkeys and has a cat named Cleo.

MISTY FORMATIONS
Betty Ranck

Samuel Ha

CANOEING AT DOW LAKE

As the car slowly comes to a screeching stop,
And the warm late summer breeze starts to fill in,
We rush out with adventure and excitement swelling inside of us,
We have a quick snack as our parents pay,
We grab canoes with fascinating designs each one saying, "Pick me!"
We push off like birds leaving their nests as the paddles hit the clear calm water,
We create ripples with intriguing patterns on the surface of the water
as our paddles dip in,
We go soaring across the vast lake as our parents struggle to keep up,
We go so fast it feels like we are racing,
We go so fast it feels like we are flying,
It's so peaceful as we reach the finish line, yet as we get off we are tired
and panting,
We start to feel sad as we get off because we know that this wonderful event
has come to a cease,
Then a shadow passes over our heads,
We look up to see a flock of birds migrating south in preparation of fall,
We get into the car as we follow the birds into the dim-lighted sunset.

Samuel Ha is a 6th grader who lives with his family in Athens, OH. He likes soccer and swimming.
He also enjoys watching the anime, Naruto, and likes to play "The Legend of Zelda Breath of the
Wild" on his Nintendo Switch. He wishes that he had a pet since he does not have one.

Anna Lachman

CHERRY TREES

Across the road the cherry trees beckon to us,
Bending and waving in the wind

A picnic spread beneath the branches,
Family sitting next to the sparkling river

A brilliant sky painted with the colors of the world fades into a soft
lavender dusk that seems to make the cherry blossoms glow

In the light of the silver moon and under the twinkling stars

Friends,

Family,

Laughing,

Loving,

Each year we are different.

Anna Lachman is in 6th grade at East Elementary. She enjoys art, baking, sewing, and
dance. She has a fluffy orange cat named Clementine, and a Siamese cat named Lulu. She
has two amazing parents and two loving sisters.

Jacob Gutekanst

THE RIDGES

The car pulls up on the icy road
We step out in our cozy gear
Grab the sleds with our thick cotton gloves,
Step by step
We slowly make our way to the top of the hill.

But once at the peak
Catching our breath, amazed at the sight
We speed down the powdery snow
Ensconced In snowflakes
Flying in our wakes

And once at the bottom
We repeat our tracks,
As to do the whole thing once again.
Oh Athens, the feel and smell
Of this beautiful place.

Jacob Gutekanst is a 6th grader in Athens, Ohio. He loves dogs, swimming, and Minecraft. He has two dogs, Cubby and Luna, and has a brother who is in high school named Sam.

Essie Cornett

SEASONS IN ATHENS

Feel the cool breeze tickle my nose,
Rush through my hair,
The smell of a campfire drifts past.
Breathe it in,
Breathe it out.

Noticing all the bright colors,
Red,
Orange,
Yellow.
Hidden in the trees,
Elm,
Buckeye,
Maple.

Snow crunches,
As the weight of our steps press upon it,
Block by block,
Brick by brick.

Collapse in my bed after a long day,
The stars glisten,
Casting light through my windows,
I drift off to sleep,
To the sound of chirping crickets.

Essie Cornett is a 6th grader at East Elementary. She enjoys baking, riding horses, and hanging out with her friends and family. She has also been doing Irish dance for over seven years and hopes to continue for as long as possible.

TORTOISE AND HARE
Keith Wilde

GOTTA LOVE LOCAL

You're walking down the street and go into the Farmer's market it's fun, perfect, and local.

You're walking down the street and go into the Kindred Market it's fun, perfect, local local.

You're walking down the street and go into the Donkey Coffee it's fun, local, local local.

You're walking down the street and go into the Casa Nueva it's local, local, local local.

You're walking down the street and go into the Village Bakery local local, local, local local.

You're walking down the street and go into local Avalanche Pizza local local, local, local local.

You're walking down the street and go local local Sol Restaurant local local, local, local local.

You're walking down the street and local local local Kennedy Museum local local, local, local local.

You're walking down the street local local local local Jackie O's local local, local, local local.

You're walking down the local local local local local O'Betty's Hot Dogs local local, local, local local.

You're walking down local local local local local local Restaurant Salaam local local, local, local local.

You're walking local local local local local local local Thai Paradise local local, local, local local.

You're local local local local local local local local Miller's Chicken local local, local, local local.

Local local local local local local local local local Athens, Ohio local local, local, local local.

As local as we can be.

Timmy Chesser is a 6th grader from Athens, Ohio. He is very athletic and plays football (favorite) and basketball. Some of his favorite hobbies are drawing, practicing football (if he's not playing), going outside, and playing videogames. He's lived in Athens for almost his whole life and wants to spend more of it in Athens

Eden Radcliff

SEASONS IN ATHENS

Summer, Summer
Warm and fun
Warm and fun for everyone!
Children run and laugh and play,
Seems like it's only been one day.

Time for fall
It's getting colder.
School starts, cool mornings, cover your shoulders.
The college kids are back in town
Makes all the adults feel so run down.

It's time for winter, now I'm done!
It's cold and wet and just no fun.
You get into your snow suit and grab your sleigh
Just because school's out today!

It's spring time at last.
All the seasons went by so fast!
You've lived another year, amen.
Now it's time to start over again.

Eden Radcliff is an eleven-year-old, 6th grade student who attends Morrison-Gordon Elementary school. She has two dogs and three cats and enjoys doing theater in her spare time. She lives in Athens, Ohio and is excited to share her poetry for the first time!

ATTACK ZOMBIE SOCK MONSTERS

Danette Pratt

ANYWHERE YOU GO

A cloudy day in Athens
Rain pats the roof of a local restaurant
Come on down to Athens it has anything you want
On the countryside with chickens and hens
Or in a cafe satisfying your cleanse
Come down to Athens rainy day or not
It will be a great time, you will miss it a lot

Roman Trout is a 6th grader at Morrison-Gordon Elementary. He loves his family and pets. He has a cat, dog, and turtle and he loves them very much. He also participates in Model United Nations. He also loves to converse.

ATHENS

The beautiful city of Athens
The rolling hills under the warmth of the sun
The soft clouds brushing against the night sky
The towering clock that rises above each day and night
The crimson red bricks that are paved along historic streets
The dedicated OU fans in every nook and cranny
The colored trees in the fall
The fast passing rapids in the hocking
The beautiful city of Athens

Emma Molde has lived in Athens for 6 years. She is 12 years old. She enjoys sports, painting, and hiking. She has one brother, a dog, and a rabbit. She attends Morrison-Gordon Elementary School.

Jeremy King

THE PLACE WHERE THE GRASS GROWS LONG

The place where the grass grows long
And the blue jays sing their quiet song
The place where the grass grows long
And we see why the war was wrong

The place where the wind sighs sad
For The Ridges are thought of as bad
The place where the wind sighs sad
For the people that had gone mad

The place where the poppies bloom
Their tasks, the solemn graves they groom
The place where the poppies bloom
Spread out to give the walkway room

The place where the grass grows long
And we see why the war was wrong
The place where the grass grows long
And the bluejays sing their quiet song
The place where the grass grows long

Jeremy King is eleven years old and lives in Athens, Ohio with his sister and parents. In his
free time he enjoys reading, playing outside, and playing Minecraft with his neighbor.

Lily Wolfe

WINTER IS REALLY HERE

The snow has fallen on the college green

It lay there softly glistening in the morning sun

Nobody is out, only indoors

The sun has risen yet it's still quite dark, the brisk air is growing colder and colder

The day passes by as if it had only been a minute

The sun starts to set and everybody stays

Everybody gathers around to look at the beautiful scene

It's as if we were in a wonderland, or some kind of beautiful fairytale, but no… it's real

Sparkling lights are scattered across the trees and buildings

Shimmering lights are almost blinding reflecting off the snow

Yet the love that surrounds us is even more blinding

And that's how we all know that winter is really here

Athens

Lily Wolfe is 12 years old and attends Morrison-Gordon Elementary school. She has three dogs, one cat and likes to paint, sketch, and cook in her spare time.

Alexander Wotschka

ATHENS

Such a nice town.
Such a beautiful town.
The birds, oh the birds just flying around.
The song, the life runs through the trees.

The life and love of this town.
Is the best all around.
We work hard for change.
And help out all over this great town of ours.

Live, Love, Laugh, Play,
All reality on an Athens summer day.
Athens,
Oh Athens.

Alexander is a 6th grader who lives in Athens. He enjoys spending time outside
and likes playing sports such as soccer and baseball. He also loves, on rainy days,
to curl up on the couch with a snack and read a nice book.

UNTITLED
Shannon Moyer

RIDING ALONG

The geese cried as we rode by,
Wind filled our ears with sighs.
The river was waving hello.

We pedaled past the people,
Speeding across a blur of green.
Yet the river was at our side.

We rose up high, then fell down low,
The laughing hills let us fly.
We dipped again, the river waved goodbye.

Lizzie Castelino is a 6th grader who attends West Elementary. She has now enjoyed the beautiful sights of Athens, Ohio for seven years.

Addie McGarry

A MAGICAL PLACE

When you are a child the world seems magical.

When you ride your bike or take a walk.

When you play outside or swim in a pool.

But nowhere was more magical to me than Strouds Run.

At Strouds Run you can see unicorns, dragons and princesses.

At Strouds Run water becomes lava, mud becomes gooey slime and trees become monsters.

But that was when I was little, though I can still see a little magic.

At Strouds Run you can see sunflowers smiling at the sun.

At Strouds Run your dogs act like puppies.

At Strouds Run you can swing like there's no tomorrow.

At Strouds Run you feel like a little kid.

Addie McGarry is a 6th grader who attends Morrison-Gordon Elementary in Athens, OH. She loves animals and nature. She is the tallest player on a basketball team with her friends and she performs in musicals in her community theater. She loves her family, friends and her pets.

THE BIKE TRAIL

They call it the Bike Trail,
But I see everything but bikes.

There are skateboards and roller skates
And scooters and tricycles.

There are some who jog and some who run
And some who sit in little strollers!

There are a number of walkers walking their dogs
And families and friends who all come together.

Yet I see not a single bike except mine.
Isn't this supposed to be the Bike Trail?

Helen Liu is a 6th grader who loves to read, write, and draw. She likes to spend time with her family and friends and play card games.

Miles Makosky

ATHENS, OHIO

With its roots deep
And its footing strong
It grows and grows
But nothing is perfect
Even here leaves can fall
yet they still bring us hope
For a new batch can grow
Again growing and growing
While spreading the love
Of this family tree

Miles Makosky is a 6th grader, Athens. OH.

BLOODROOT

Tim Creamer

I SEE PLACES

I take the bike path along the river

But I have to pause

For water starts to fall in small drops from the sky

I drive gently and smooth

Through the damp atmosphere

As I drive further into town

I see places

Water splashes up on the paved road as we drive through the town

Ben Kessler is a 6th grader who lives with his parents and his 15-year-old brother in Athens, Ohio. He goes to Morrison-Gordon Elementary and every Thursday he goes to the Gifted Pull Out Program. He likes playing as well as watching sports such as basketball and baseball.

ATHENS DREAMLAND

My feet splash in the water
And even though it's spring
My face is red and upset
I can't keep my head from aching

My feet splash in the water
Maybe just to get away
To find a peaceful refuge
Where I'm positive I'll stay

My feet splash in the water
But then I stop where I stand
Because I see the perfect spot
My absolute dreamland

My feet splash in the water
I sit on the soft, green moss
At my peaceful destination
I feel zero loss

My feet splash in the water
My eyes wander all around
I see butterflies flap their colorful wings
And caterpillars crawling on forest ground

My feet splash in the water
Now finally I'm here
Athens is the perfect place
I produce a single tear

Lucy Ingram is 12 years old and attends Morrison-Gordon Elementary. She likes
animals and has one cat and a bulldog. She loves summer and enjoys nature and being
outside. Lucy likes to read, paint, draw, play with her dog, cook, and enjoys many other
activities in her free time.

RIDGES COLLAGE
Brytton Jarrett

Robin Schaffer

I MADE UP MY MIND TO MARRY THIS TOWN

The moon seems closer here
in Appalachia— and I can be
an unpretentious woman.
Green trees cover me, cozy—
and the hills wrap around
the town.

At the Blue Eagle music store
friends play scrabble, slipping
in a few Vietnamese words.
Young musicians lean on the pot-
belly stove, sucking up lines
of old-time songs. Voices merge
like gentle currents of the
Hocking River.

A unicycle rider with a Rip Van Winkle
beard whirls down State Street
like a bird in the air.
A favorite high-heeled singer
still shakes her straight hair
and a fine guitar man spins out
his songs of vivid poetry.

On Saturdays, I carry my ancient
basket to the farmers market.
Once I found a parsnip with
more arms than a sea monster.
Summer tomatoes are luscious
in purples and stripes of yellows.
I love the sweet golden beets
and peaches in mid-summer.

Halloween is always riotous.
Once there was a bodacious roller ghost
gliding on skates and faith. It was dark and

he waited at the top of Court Street.
Thousands of revelers paved the way like Moses
parting the Red Sea. The ghost flew past Union Street,
then Washington —the cheering was ear-splitting.
He flew by State Street to the music stage,
guitars on reverb, the crowd was frenzied.

Giant puppets parade on Court Street,
dressed up in sparkle paint, paper maché
fantasies, counterfeit hair flying as high
as the roof tops and kids climb up
on their Daddy's shoulders.
Neighbors at Casa, arguing out
the rights or the wrongs while
breakfast slides onto midday lunch.
Most of us are like-minded anyway.

Neon lights in the windows of Tony's Bar
flash when it rains, shimmer like stars
in yellows and blues drizzling
on the bricks, the color of dark
red lipstick. I dance with the lights
on wet streets— sweet dreams
in my sleep.

Tom Quinn

IN THE QUIET

I squeeze her hand gently
Not for fear of pain
But to simply acknowledge.
Let her know I'm aware of her quiet presence.
Enjoying the moment
Our moment.
Her eyes found mine
And she smiled.

A-TOWN FROM BONG HILL
Tina Shoup

TWO OF US ON THE RUN

My little brown bulldog and I arrived in Athens, Ohio, late in the evening of April 29, 2016.

I pulled my rusty '06 Nissan to the curb of 60 Central, a crooked house with moldy siding in a neighborhood full of crooked houses with moldy siding, unkept lawns, and Tibetan prayer flags. My dog, (whose full name was Agatha but whom I had nicknamed Bag,) trotted after me and I unlocked the door to our new home: its slanting floors and stained carpet and warped walls welcoming us.

We started unpacking my things, losing ourselves in deteriorating cardboard boxes of records, CDs, and a raggedy collection of books. With no air conditioner the work became sticky and arduous in the early hours of the morning and I rinsed myself in the shower before falling into a hard sleep, Bag curled up at my side.

The next morning I awoke in a panic, uncertain of where I was. I opened my eyes and the stained ceiling of my new abode greeted me, the midday sun illuminating the crusty carpet and middle of my thinning bedspread. I saw Bag, still asleep, snoring, her deep, labored breaths flapping through her thick lips laying in the midst of a sunbeam pouring from my bedroom window.

Only weeks prior, moving south had been a pipe dream. I had been the editor of a newspaper in the heart of Ohio Amish Country, a free weekly that arrived every Monday on the steps of homes throughout the tri-county area, whether they wanted it or not.

Back then I was 23. I was very alone, and I was very scared.

He was a musician, and that should have been warning enough. Of course, things had seemed rather grand after I first met him – it was only after he had brought his things into my home and convinced me that I shouldn't let anyone know about it that he hit me for the first time.

His violence became frequent and unpredictable. If I clattered the silverware too much while putting it away, if I was too frantic in my vacuuming, if I spoke too loudly – I did not know when his blows would come but they almost always would.

When the dubious possibility of a part time job at a public radio station that I had volunteered at as a student came into the picture, I began formulating my escape plan. I took my things, one box at a time, to my parent's home and hoarding them in my childhood bedroom.

In the middle of the night that March he shook me awake for the last time. While we screamed at each other, I tossed clothes into a bag. He grabbed my arms, but this time I was seething, and with some kind of unknown strength, I swatted him away and spat at him -- running to my car and barreling my way through the early spring darkness to my parent's house, where I lived for the last two weeks of my time up north.

I gave my parents few details, other than I was working on getting a job in Athens, and that I would take them up on their constant offer of a dog. My mother is veterinarian, and I grew up in a home with no shortage of pets. She gave me Agatha. She was seven years old, had birthed many puppies, and was reportedly moody and aggressive.

The day I accepted the job in Athens my mother spayed Bag, and that night Bag recuperated in a kennel in my parent's kitchen. After everyone had drifted off to their separate quarters, I came downstairs and opened Bag's kennel door and I laid down with her – weeping.

After I moved, I did not know how quickly things would change for Bag and me.

I did not know the ease with which I would begin to sing to myself again, how I would start to playfully warble my voice to match the tone of the synthesizers in my favorite songs. I felt myself thawing, with every sunlit walk in my recently deserted college town in early summer. My voice became louder, like an AM dial landing on the right frequency.

In time, I stopped looking over my shoulder. On our walks, Bag and I would traipse sidewalks broken by the waxing and waning of time, stalwart dandelions creeping through the cracks in the cement. Bag became soft, cuddly – her aggression fading to the point of being imperceptible.

Summer loped on.

I made friends. I'd walk home in syrupy darkness after a night of revelry, my heart suspended like a bug in brandy. The disintegrating houses and the pungent scent of summer seemed to coalesce into something deeply beautiful all around me – the overwhelming chorus of the cicadas that summer vibrating through the streets I walked home on. The tree in the front of my apartment sprang to life, it's formerly barren branches heavy with white flowers by mid-June.

Sometimes I would think of my former life –I found myself pruning ornamental memories, psychologically packing them into tidier and tidier boxes so that everything else would have room to grow.

I worked multiple jobs in addition to the one I moved for: lying about my accounting abilities to snag a short-lived job at a student housing agency; a particularly poignant term as an assistant at a children's drama camp; an oddly pleasant number of months spent as a grocery store cashier. In the darkness of the winters that followed, I would hold Bag close at night in the clamminess of baseboard heating, reminding myself over and over that I needed to only keep one foot in front of the other.

Shortly after I received the promotion to full-time and could quit those aforementioned second jobs, a chance encounter with a stranger with eyes like melted chocolate blossomed into a romance – one that we would seal with a small ceremony in Stroud's Run some years after my arrival in Athens.

My little brown bulldog and I sleep soundly these days, and we wake rested. We no longer live in the little neighborhood with the slanting rooftops and the moldy siding, but sometimes we dream of it and that golden, Athenian summer wherein we assembled ourselves.

MUSICAL MELDING
Tim Creamer

Jared A. Butcher, Jr.

DETECTIVE-POET SOUGHT

The scene opens to reveal a gray-haired man in a gray suit wearing a gray tie. He is sitting at his desk when an assertive knock assails his door. He does not rise. He does not jump. He exudes—if that's a word—loudly as he speaks:

Mr. Gray: Come in.

Miss Born enters. She is wearing a long brown dress tight fitting to the knee and then expanding to a flounce. Her shoes tap as she walks, lifting her feet without bending anything. (This produces a humorously melodious clopping sound set to the tune of "Popcorn:" "Top, top, top, top, top, top, top, top... Top, top, top, top, top, top, top, top..." She arrives at the open chair and stands behind it, bending one knee as if in an effort to stop the nuisance clopping.

Miss Born: Miss Born.
Mr. Gray: F.N. Born?
Miss Born: Precisely. 'Miss F.N. Born.'
Mr. Gray: Yes, and what can I do for you? Miss Born?
Miss Born: Oh, my dear sir, it is what I can do for you.
Mr. Gray: For--me?
Miss Born: I have been given to understand that you are looking
                for a story about a detective-poet.
Mr. Gray: Ah... You know a detective-poet?
Miss Born: My father, W.W. Fardels Bear.
Mr. Gray: I've never heard of him. What has he done?
Miss Born: Nothing. You would gain credit for discovering
                new talent.
Mr. Gray: Talented detective-poet, you say--who has done
                nothing... Let's hear one of his poems--a short poem--if
                you please.
Miss Born: "O F B, it was he... Mr. Gray, you must know that FB is
                short for Fardels Bear. 'Fardels Bear' is simply too long to...
Mr. Gray: Enough with the story. Let's have the poem.
Miss Born: "O F B, it was he--sitting 'neath the old dead tree--feeling
                stung upon the 's--he stood straight up and said: 'Ex Lax.'"
Mr. Gray: Why did he say that? It doesn't rhyme.
Miss Born: Uh--mm--uh.. That isn't what he said.

Mr. Gray:	What did he say?
Miss Born:	Um… That…didn't rhyme, either.
Mr. Gray:	I see. So, this Mister Bear is an undiscovered…
Miss Born:	Herr Bear.
Mr. Gray:	What?
Miss Born:	It's 'Herr Bear' when it's not 'Fardels.'
Mr. Gray:	So… "Herr Bear is an undiscovered detective-poet." That might be interesting. Does he have some use for poetry in his detective work, or is it all as useless as that last little ditty?

Miss Born does not like Mr. Gray's tone. She stands up clops around behind her chair and scrapes it along the floor until it puts her within striking distance of Mr. Gray, stamps her foot, then clops around and sits down. Mr. Gray takes note.

Mr. Gray:	Err. (strangled)
Miss Born:	Sir, I think you need to understand. Where Fardels Bear is concerned, poetry is power. Poetry puts meaning in the meaningless. Poetry provides clues to the clueless, knowledge to the know it all. Let me explain:
Mr. Gray:	If you must.
Miss Born:	In that case, I insist. As you doubtless know, I work for Mrs. Virginia West. She manages the affairs for a small…
Mr. Gray:	Yes, yes, I know all that. I read your resume already.
Miss Born:	Then, you know that Virginia is the mother of four.
Mr. Gray:	No. I missed that part…
Miss Born:	I thought as much. Well, on the Fourth of July, she and a group of her friends were celebrating when one of the other children wet its pants and her mother didn't have a change of clothes. Virginia gave her a spare pair of pants she had brought for her children. She started to put the soiled pants in her bag, and when the mother objected, Virginia said: "It's just pee."
Mr. Gray:	Fascinating. (sarcastically)
Miss Born:	Then, in our meeting, Virginia was explaining how it is our job to teach teachers what is important, and I said, "like bring spare clothes; and, 'it's just pee.'"
Mr. Gray:	(clucking sound)
Miss Born:	Virginia said: "Miss Born, I just can't imagine how your mind works." I said: "'I speak the truth in spite of my

youth and never capture much attention; I experience mirth
for what it is worth, and no one's pleased with my invention."

Mr. Gray: That's funny. What did Ms. West say to that?

Miss Born: She said, "What? Are you using poetry on us?"

*The scene changes: Mr. Gray's mind steps into the mind of Miss Born—Born
again, some might say. He sees the nuclear reactor; an alien nest curls around
it. There is the hiss of steam. As the crew walks, their feet make the sound of
walking in Jell-O®. A voice comes through the transponder:*

Central: No armor piercing rounds.

Vasquez: What do they want us to use on them? Poetry?

*The scene changes: The outside of the Nakatomi Building shudders and
shakes; windows blow out in all directions; the boom of an explosions shakes
the earth.*

Fritz: They are using poetry on us!

Hans: Not 'them,' you idiot. It's 'him.'

*Fritz morphs into an alien with its mouth open—the inner head protrudes—it
opens its mouth and screams pitiably:*

Alien: Not poetry! Not again.

The scene changes back: Ripley lounges seductively in front of the console.

Ripley: (sexy voice) Some poet we missed?

*The scene goes black and white—colors fall away with a thud: Sam Spade
bends down to pick up "the bundle." His secretary speaks:*

Effie: (Breathlessly) What is it, Sam?

Sam: This dingus? Thoreau pencils--pencil lead--the stuff that poetry
is made of...

Mr. Gray: (Howling) Miss Born, you are a mess. This story of yours...
It has me laughing more than I should when I am at work.

Miss Born looks at Mr. Gray in a new light; blue—it resembles the blue of the sky—"cerulean," I think they call it; and she sees Fardels Bear, and how Fardels Bear made his name trying to be a detective. Mr. Gray doesn't see it, so she tells it to him, but it isn't a story, really, it's: "Long and Dull." I'll read it to you, in voice, if I can manage it. (FB (book), Father (book) and Son (book) step to the microphones.)

FB (book): Long and Dull? Sounds more like the description of a shovel than the name of a law firm.

Father (book): You tryin' to make some sort of statement, or is that just an observation.

FB (book): Just an observation, I guess.

Son (book): What the h- is he talkin' about? Shovels?

Father (book): Never you mind, son.

Son (book): No. I just want to know what everybody else knows. That's all. You know what he means; I want to know what he means.

FB (book): Look, kid, if he understood half of what I have to say, he wouldn't have to be in this line of work.

Son (book): Dad? What's he talkin' about? Tell me what he's talkin' about.

Father (book): Oh, he's just talking out of his head, that's all. You'll learn: He's an idiot, doesn't make sense even half the time.

Son (book): But the shovel, Dad.

Father (book): I guess that he was sayin' that he's not too sharp. You know, dull.

Son (book): That's not what he was sayin', Dad. Dull is the word you'd use to describe a knife, not a shovel. What did you mean? Mister?

FB (book): It was a joke. I never explain a joke; so, forget it, kid.

Father (book): See? I told you.

Son (book): Okay. I guess, but I never forget a thing I don't understand.

FB (book): Good. You're a good boy. You'll grow up into a good man, and a devoted husband, with an attitude like that.

Son (book): You're makin' a joke out of me, now, aren't you.

FB (book): Whatever you say, kid.

Son (book): Dad?

Father (book): Just forget it. Leave him be.

Son (book): Mister, do you mean to say that I won't understand women?

FB (book): That's what I mean: A devoted husband doesn't forget his woman.

Son (book): Wow. I've never talked to anyone who talks like you do.

100

FB (book):	English is a fine language. You should learn it.
Father (book):	Leave him be, son. Leave him be.
Son (book):	I can't. I've got to know about the shovel.
Father (book):	You're diggin' yourself in deeper on that one, son. Leave it.
Son (book):	What do you say, Mister?
FB (book):	I speak the truth, in spite of youth, and never capture much attention. I experience mirth, for what it is worth, But no one's pleased with my invention.
Father (book):	S-! Poetry now. Kid, I told you to leave him alone. Now get out of here ! Leave him alone.

Son (book) shrugs, leaves, and slams the door.

Father (book):	You enjoy makin' life difficult? Or does it just come natural?
FB (book):	Life's difficult. I try to make it interesting.
Father (book):	A shovel that's long and dull isn't interesting.
FB (book):	No, but it might be if it was a long-handle shovel, especially, if you have a law office out digging up dirt.
Father (book):	G-! You're a comedian. Too bad you aren't starvin' to death from tryin' to make a livin' at it rather than devilin' me and the boy with your conundrums.
FB (book):	Big word, 'conundrums'; be careful how you use it.
Father (book):	Stick it!
FB (book):	Never without a conundrum. The kid's still stuck and so were you.
Father (book):	You know what I meant.
FB (book):	Yeah, I always know what you meant. Too bad you can't say the same for me.
Father (book):	Okay. So what have you found out? And give it to me plain Ican't take any more conundrums. Things are already pretty ...
FB (book):	Uh, uh, uh. None of that. The language has taken enough insults from you already. No need to add to it... Here's what I've got.
Miss Born:	FB had a real report, of course, but I'll leave it out here.
Son (book):	Uh, Sir? Mister
FB (book):	What?
Son (book):	It could just as easily of been underwear or a screwdriver.
FB (book):	What?

Son (book):	Your joke, Sir: 'Long and Dull'.
FB (book):	Oh, that. How long did it take you? Or did somebody tell you.
Son (book):	No sir. It hit me just as the door closed behind me.
FB (book):	You're pretty quick.
Son (book):	Now you're being sarcastic... I just never expected it to be a joke. It isn't right and it isn't fair.
FB (book):	That's a racist riddle, and sexist for my taste.
Son (book):	Oh, gross, Sir! Where did that come from? Did you decide that on the spur of the moment?
FB (book):	No. I heard that riddle in a movie one time, long time ago.
Son (book):	You remember everything you ever heard in a movie?
FB (book):	No, only the stuff that appeals to my peculiar sense of humor.
Son (book):	'Peculiar' doesn't cover it. Do you always obscure your ideas under a veneer of humor?
FB (book):	Sure. It gives me my edge, my advantage. It puts my listener on his guard - makes him aware...
Son (book):	That you're a pretty smart cookie.
FB (book):	'Smarter than the average bear.' That's what my high school English teacher told me... I told her that even if I was 'smarter than the average bear', I was still a bear... might make a good pseudonym: 'Grizzly Bear'.
Son (book):	No. I think you need something with more teeth in it.
FB (book):	You find me scary? I'm actually a pretty scary once you get to know me.
Son (book):	The jokes make knowing you impossible, but I can tell you already, scary as you are, you'll never be pretty.
FB (book):	Thanks a bunch, kid.
Son (book):	You're welcome, and another thing: It's Long and Duhl: It's pronounced 'duel' as in D-U-E-L: Long and Duhl.
FB (book):	(snorts) Boring.

Miss Born looks up from her reading. Mr. Gray sits with his head in his hands. His eyes are closed; a tear hangs from the tip of his nose. He takes a tissue from his pocket and blows his nose into it before speaking:

Mr. Gray:	I don't know, Miss... That wasn't a poem, and it wasn't a story, really. Quite frankly, I don't think it was much of anything.

crowd: (off duty actors embedded in the audience boo and hiss--encouraging the actual audience to do the same.)

Mr. Gray:	Look, guys, you're killing me. I've got two words for you: 'Anton Webern'--like 'Weber' with an 'n.' Look that up on your smart phone while I finish up here, will you?
Miss Born:	So, why did you advertise for a 'detective-poet' when you didn't really want one?
Mr. Gray:	I'm sorry. What were you saying? I was a little distracted there for a moment.
Miss Born:	So, why did you advertise for a 'detective-poet?'
Mr. Gray:	To see if there was one.
Miss Born:	Just to see?
Mr. Gray:	Yes. I have found chemist-poets, engineering-poets, mathematician-poets, not very good: "My love for you will never die. My love exceeds one over y, as y approaches zero..." It seems that anyone seeking order in their life, turns to poetry... So why not a detective?
Miss Born:	So, Mr. Gray, are you seeking order in your life?
Mr. Gray:	Um... Why do you ask?
Miss Born:	I wonder if you are a poet.
Mr. Gray:	I, uh... I dabble a little.
Miss Born:	So, let's hear some of your dabbling.
Mr. Gray:	My favorite is "The day after beautiful weather." The day after beautiful weather, suffering students take exams together; the weather is cold... No. The teacher is old; the weather is cold; but the exam is impossible as ever ... on the day after... Go on. Get out of here.
Miss Born:	So-o, you are a teacher? What do you teach?
Mr. Gray:	Chemistry.
Miss Born:	'Chemist-poet.' What kind of chemistry?
Mr. Gray:	Organic.
Miss Born:	Ooh: Organic chemistry--it's a bear. (Sniffs)

Miss Born turns on her heel and clops out of the room to the rhythm of "Popcorn" and slams the door behind her as the actual song comes up.

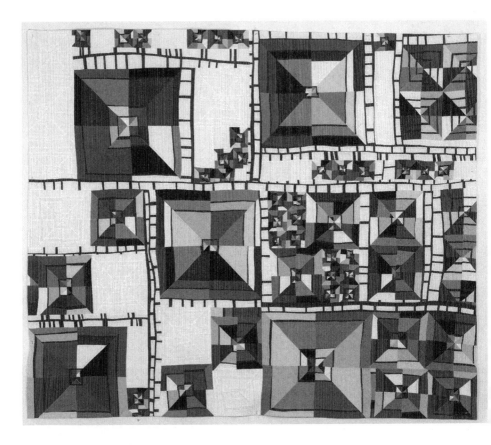

LINE STUDY 17
Margaret Black

Joseph Shumar (Federal Hocking Middle School)

I AM FROM

I'm from the maple, oak, hickory, spruce
and pine trees in the unnamed woods.
I am the deer, rabbits, squirrels, snakes, birds,
and coyotes living in the woods.
I am the stump that is surrounded by dirt,
glass bottles, and the creek.
I am the creek that provides vegetation
and water for the animals in the woods.
I am from the ghostly whisper of trees,
animals, creek, and vegetation.

I'm from the dirt roads.
I am from country.
I am from people called rednecks and hillbillies.
I am from people who dislike city-slickers.
I am from people who know how and can live off the land.

I'm from those hunters and fishers
who only kill to feed their families.
I am from the rocks in my driveway
that I used to lick.
I am from the woods I know and love.
I am the unnamed woods.

Steve Zarate

SIGHT FOR SORE EYES

When she first appears,
    after time away,
She's the breath of fresh air
    in the smoke-filled room,
A patch of daisies
    climbing through asphalt
Melody snaking through chaos,
    the diamond in the rough.

Coming from the north
    you traverse a valley.
A river winds, hills roll,
    ordinary prevails, as it must.
Bypassing an exit you climb,
    cresting a high hill,
Only to descend toward her beauty,
    where ordinary
    subsides.

From other directions, the same:
    roads, twisting, turning and opening
Into her tableau vivant,
    that same river semi-circling her
    curved slopes,
Long-time dance partner,
    ocean-bound but
    here for now.

At night, her lights twinkling,
    shimmering across its surface,
    wild geese-chaperoned,
The liquid thoroughfare hugs her,
    then lets go. Her townspeople
Dream, then rise to inhabit
    extraordinary streets.
In wooded farmlands,
    for miles around,
Coyotes howl into the dark,
    wishing for a taste
    of her sparkle.

ODE TO ATHENS

We are from rolling hills,
from Starbricks and Passion Flowers.

We are from company towns,
pride, grit, fresh-tilled earth.

We're from paw-paws,
brewed, baked, celebrated.

We're from 30 Mile Meal
and locally owned,
from Ada Adams and the Brooks family,
from tenacity and resilience.

We're from open arms,
open minds, authentic smiles.

We're from coal, iron, higher education,
from the Burrito Buggy, Casa Nueva
and great pizza, from the
simple kindness of Margaret McGrainer
to the courage of the Courier sisters.

We are from connections
and thriving community centers,
where our history lives on
in each other.

OUT HARMONY WAY

I live in a place just outside of town,
but can feel a whole world away. Away from the people and the parties.
I live in a place where I can still hear the highway. But I can hear coyotes
and owls and hawks and herons, because compromise is the spice of life.
I live in a place that floods and forces me to hike out the ridge to get to
town. I get to see animal tracks and wildflowers, and pump blood and heat
into my machine of a body.
I live in a place where I can walk down the road in the dark, in the rain,
and feel safe and alone. The frogs and the salamanders feel it, too.
I live in a place of privilege.
I live in a place that's a gift.

Stephanie Kendrick

ATHENS, OHIO: A LOVE STORY

Summer
Under the heat of July we walk along the Hocking River,
listening for the secrets kept under her stagnant film.
We are a town who talks with cellos, smoke
and newspaper letters. Our words are ripped apart and buried
in the hills with the rest of the dark matter
that finds its way back to the water, rusty.
Wiping away our sweat, we pause. Looking into
the still stream, hushed and glistening-
we are tempted to stick our feet in. Desperate,
to wash away the heat.

Autumn
He takes my hand and says –"Is there anything more gorgeous
than Athens in the fall?" and of course, this is true-
To question if anything else could be as perfect.
Even as the ironweed fades,
its intense purple slowly drying into beige, signaling its death-
I lose my breath.
I squeeze his palm and pray for the same transcendence.

Winter
We drift through winter like dandelion seeds.
Migrating geese rest on ice plates
that form on our quiet river. A midafternoon sun
reflects off of the snow, blinding. We wrap
ourselves so tightly into each other's stories
that we no longer see the steam from our breath.

Spring
The Hocking thrashes, spilling her secrets.
He grabs my waist and kisses my nose in the rain-whispers something
about a fresh start. And I find my breath
spreading through the hills like kudzu.
The dandelions bloom in the wet grass and blue jays yell from their nests.
The River carries with her the dead and thawing stories left unfinished
and heavy. We are a town who talks
with food, side-eyes and overflowing charity.
Our stories as layered as our hills
and as wild as our river.

Maura Kennedy Anaya

MY FIRST NIGHT IN ATHENS, OHIO

was the week of winter exams
My long-held husband
earnest tour guide
enthusing me about
restaurants on Court Street

I threadbare
from dismantling a full life
Stunned by the fact
I live here now

was suddenly captured
by the faces
dotting the street brighter
more beautiful than
they will realize for years

The spring in each step
vibrating the bricks
Hives of youth

Nostalgia
struck me down

Remembering
the anticipation spilling out
Back when my to do list
was full of novelty

Before he was a husband
he had that same look
Fueled by tequila
the moment
before he kissed me
the first time

Svenn Lindskold

PEACE AT ONE'S FINGERTIPS

A young man – he had a heavy book bag,
so he must have been a student – leaned over
and stroked and gently felt the lazy bones of the cat
lying on the sidewalk, taking in the sunshine.
The man leaned over again, and then again, to touch
and to sense the calm and peace of the sun-warm cat:
comfortable, enjoying the day, the earth, his peace with it.

The young man thought of the Russian revolution,
about which he had just been reading, and he thought
of more current times. Where is the peace
so available to this symbolic cat on this sunny afternoon?
Where is the peace in the Middle East, in the meeting
rooms of the nation's capital, among neighbors on this street,
at the frontiers of grasping, discontented peoples?

It is so easy – the peace of this cat –
the warmth of sunshine, stopping
to stroke a loving, appreciative being
that knows luxury and tranquility
and security among others without having
a big house, a big car, a big bank account
or an audience of fools fawning over him --
fools not knowing what they want because, unlike
the sunshine on this sidewalk, it is all too complicated.

The young man, seeking peace,
leaned over once again
and reached to stroke the welcoming cat.

Violeta Orozco

THE PLACE ON THE OTHER SIDE OF THE HOCKING

I strive for the sight of the place in my mind
A river in Ohio close to where I lived
I begin to remember
The river ringing in my ears, a frozen space
Where the water used to chime
Time caught between corn ears
A lazy drop falling slowly through the seasons
The wild geese rising from the bridge
The beach in the middle of the forest at Strouds
Switching from blue to brown, brown to black to bloom
A photograph slipped across the chain of hands
A deer leaping across the colors
Strange words ringing in the landscape by the tracks
Of the bygone trains a trail
Of stones and metal piercing into the forest
Rock Caves hanging out the hocking hills
But no river
No track of the mud fled wing
I know there was a water bed a water body
I know there was a body whispering out its shape
To someone
Seven years ago
Why?
Should I say five months so the pain is less?
Little did I know of the reality of knives
That cut me up the ax
That made air thin with pain
All that had been whole was now a howl
I thought I was the old lady inside
The one who stared out at the tracks
Fell in love with the river and the rain
Their hypnotizing movement resembling her own pace
As she swept back and forth across the room
The fireplace quietly blazing in her eyes
A twin agony in the Athenian night
Oh for all I know I could have burnt away

Blown away
Borne away
Like the house in the three little pigs thrice destructed
As my resurrection boasts.
But I did not die at the same time.
I died before the river, the forest and the train.

Alyssa R. Bernstein

WHY EVEN TRY TO BEAUTIFY

Athens, Ohio is a town where people try to beautify things.
Not everybody, of course.
And you might think, if you love seeing wildflowers,
meandering rivers, and forested hills
with trees that bloom in spring and summer,
that there's no need to make extra efforts here, and
that people should spend their time doing other things.

But I wasn't talking about planting flowers and painting murals,
although there are multicolored gardens on the traffic islands,
each unique, some whimsical, others geometric,
there is a two-story mural of swooping butterflies
that greets traffic entering town from the northeast,
further south a huge painted dove looks you in the eye
while the rest of its bevy flies across a wall of blues
shading from periwinkle to summer-morning azure,
lit-up photos brighten the municipal parking garage,
striking murals pay tribute to laborers,
huge painted sunflowers climb up a home's back wall
while real ones down the street grow two storys high,
not to mention the whimsical or geometric
multicolored gardens around people's homes
or the grove of Japanese cherry trees by the river
that bloom in spring.

No, I was talking about the people.
So many of them, despite living with difficulties,
are courteous, friendly, and generous.
Maybe I notice this especially because
I'm not from here.
I grew up in one of the biggest, busiest cities.
Or maybe I notice it because I've gone through hard times
of various kinds, early and late in my life.
I know that many of the people around here
try to beautify things for each other and for everyone
because they know how hard life can be.
I appreciate this, and I am thankful.

Emily Prince

CHANGE

Since we're reflecting, I'm thinking about the day when, just for a minute we were Americans. Not flag-waving, gun-toting, big-truck-lovers, but people who understood country as a concept, not a place.

I'm thinking about change. I'm thinking about all the ways that I'm different than I was the day before. Little things I still do that I didn't do before, like carry a lot of stuff, for emergencies.

I remember the feel of the air and the color of the sky and I'm filled with terror when I feel that air and see that sky again. And, I remember the smell, when the wind changed.

I'm thinking about how it wasn't the first time I heard my dad cry but it was the first time I heard him cry about me when he asked me to come home. So I thought about how in 1981 I couldn't sleep because I was afraid of Mount St. Helen erupting until my mom told me that I didn't have to worry because we lived in Ohio and we didn't have volcanos, or tidal waves, or disasters, and that as long as I stayed in Ohio I'd be safe and that I should have listened.

Then I think about how other humans right now experience that day everyday, and I feel selfish.

I still believe we can be better than what small minded people turned that day into–because we were, if only for a minute.

ANGELS (SONG)

Oh my head's spinning around
Cause there's so many pretty girls in town
Like the ones looking at me now

My face is always beat red
And sinful thoughts run through my head
And I simply ask how

So many sweethearts ended up at my back door
Everywhere I go my jaw drags on the floor
No room for concentration, in this newfound salvation
I've never seen angels before

I'm making my way through Athens
With my heart in my hand
I'm making my way through Athens
Where it's difficult to stand

When you're a simple commoner
And everywhere you turn there's a queen

I'm making my way through Athens
Heart rate 203
I'm making my way through Athens
Where it's difficult to breathe

My confidence was stolen
By the girls that I see in my dreams

Oh my head's spinning around
Cause I'm in heaven and I won't come down
My feet won't ever touch the ground

Smart, ambitious, and dorky
Fashionistas, and sporty
I was lost, but now I'm forever found

My heart skips a beat when I see them smile
Enchanting pearly eyes shine for miles
They overflow with beauty. They shine like stars in the sky
I need to find a job so I can stay a little while

I'm making my way through Athens
With my heart in my hand
I'm making my way through Athens
Where it's difficult to stand

When you're a simple commoner
And everywhere you turn there's a queen

I'm making my way through Athens
Heart rate 203

AN INVITATION TO MY SISTER

Jane, don't be afraid
to drive down those roads through towns
with all of their Biblical names,
like Canaan and Gahanna.
Some lands open up like a Bible.

Some freeways hum to the hills
merging welcome with farewell,
past fields that box into bales
squeeze and dry cut the wind.

The trinket moon's sparkle
in the rear view mirror
can't compete with all those
baubles of headlights.

The radio invites you back,
so just go.
Steely Dan's crooning.
Is there gas in the car?

Yes, there's gas in the car.

You were made for better things,
after all, stuffing cake
into the mouth of your man
on the day of your wedded bliss.
Now, you turn worries on struts.

As we bust out of our old dresses
fashioned by our mother
stitched up with bluebirds
red at the breast
blue at the bottom
wet hems against our legs.

Fevers solved with bath salts
handfuls into water
smelling of flowers.
Thermometers stuck up our butts
like we were ducks, patted
to dry, steaming, too juicy to prick.

Along every roadway
Chicory, that exhausted flower
waves its flag at us,
with ragged petals
blue flames kept low.
Pick them, they will die
in your hand, wilting like birds.

Who knew the humiliation
we would feel,
the embarrassment over stories
of our youth fading
like tarnished sumac
along the face of some mountain.

They'd say we were fast
in those days, but everything
Oh everything!
feels so damned slow
like an empty road
That will never end.

THE SYMBOLIC NATURE OF PETS

I opened a 33-gallon garbage bag,
pried your frozen body from the bottom of the boat
and dropped you into the sack like a metal shank.
I considered a proper burial, similar to those
the others had enjoyed from their distance:
candles lit, the children reciting imaginary prayers,
a grave marker -- probably a painted rock.
But it was winter this time, and you had been buried once already
beneath the ice where you died, where my husband plunged
his sober hands into the hole you fell through in the dark,
your small body shocked into experience and too late.
My daughter slept where the two of us wept for you the night before,
where I held her as if she were still a child rather than a woman;
unlike then, she feigned comfort in my arms.
Years later, it would seem as real as you once did.
You were lighter than garbage but more difficult
to carry down the lane.
Your frozen head hit my calf.
I could feel it, joyless, swirl away and back again
until, finally, I laid you in the plastic can,
positioned you between discarded gift wrap,
closed the lid. Amen.
Had Smith Hauling remained on schedule despite the holiday,
you would have made your way up Gura Road when it was ten below.
Instead, you waited through forty-degree temperatures for another week,
and I walked the dog a dozen times past you, recalling
the night you died, the morning I carried you like a repugnant stranger,
like shame, like something I have yet to say out loud.

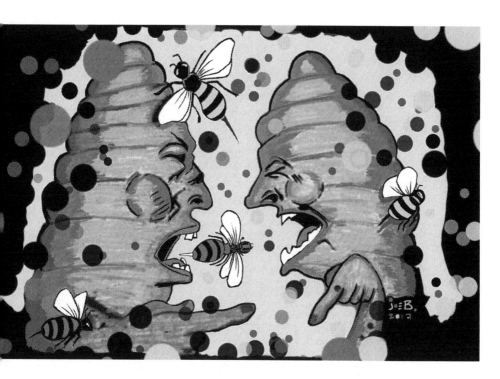

HIVE TALK
Joe Brumfield

Bruce Dalzell

THE LONG WAY HOME (SONG)

Brucie's taking the long way home tonight
Fast down the river road like a car there in flight
He's looking for something in the day's dwindling light
He's taking the long way home

Brucie's taking the long way home again
The twinkling of the Pleiades gonna lead him up around the bend
Past the coal slag and the company shacks and Willie's Dew Drop Inn
He's taking the long way home again

Brucie's taking the long way home this time
A moon so bright you could kill the lights and just drive blind
The breeze through the open window is heavy with scent of cut pine
He's taking the long way home this time

Bruce's taking the long way home it seems
He used to love to drive these back roads for miles in his teens
Drinking Stroh's and talking girls and war and everything in-between
He's taking the long way home it seems

Bruce's taking the long way home once
He's haunted by memories he really doesn't want to explore
Like the first time with Jenny on her grandmother's bathroom floor

Bruce's taking the long way home tonight
He's been wrestling demons and growing tired of the fight
But when he sees the lights of home he knows all will be right
Taking the long way home

BRICKS

Uneven bricks, tripping hazards,
ancient history. A bum prying
half-smoked cigarettes
from the cracks between.
Channels for rain, for spilled drinks,
for vomit to run its external course.
I see the bum at free lunch,
quiet and without chagrin.
I see the same people I saw
ten years ago, in the same places.
Among the swarm of transient faces,
there are hardly-noticed constants
and always will be.
It's these constants that
make it sacred, unseen to most.
Like the bricks, they can always
be found. You don't even
have to look very far.
You just have to look.

MOUNTAINS ON HER SHOULDERS

I have been lucky enough in my life to be surrounded by strong women who are, as my mom affectionately calls them, "workhorses." They have loved me, guided me, and more often than not, put me back on the right path. I have gone to them with joy and sadness and they have empathized with every moment as if it were their own. Traditions like home-cooked meals, family gatherings, grit and endurance, and pride in work, have been passed down through female generations to me. I am blessed and grateful.

But, these women also raised me to think for myself and I see other traditions and patterns that many women in my life have suffered: martyrdom for the greater good of the family, lack of self-care, and the weight of worry.

As I creep closer to my mid-forties, I find it hard to keep up with the gendered demands of an Appalachian past that, when I was younger, seemed the norm. I am a self-professed Appalachian feminist: a woman that often straddles two worlds--traditional and progressive; a woman who struggles to maintain tradition while refusing oppressive parts of it at the same time.

Vivid memories of family meals throughout my childhood include women in the kitchen fixing huge meals and then letting everyone eat before them. While this practice came from feeding the men and farmhands first because of their physical labor, there always seemed to me to be a physical sacrifice in the act of cooking the meal itself, not to mention the clean up afterward.

I've watched women in my family care for others in their community by cooking meals, volunteering time, and often giving money they can't really spare to those who need it. Altruism runs deep like the rivers in the hollers, and there is no want for recognition and accolades. These things are just what you do--you help one another in times of need.

Take a look at an Appalachian woman and you will see a proud, independent, self-reliant person. But, what you may not see are the mountains on her shoulders--mountains of worry for her children, her partner, her land, her community, her welfare, her future. It is a stoic existence that I have observed--one that often wreaks havoc on her physical body and her emotional and mental stability. She carries the weight of her world at times, often having to defend her home from outsiders who judge and stereotype Appalachia and the people in it. There are hard truths she must reckon with, both about herself and the region in which she lives.

As an Appalachian woman in 2019, I am attempting to merge two worlds. I love to cook and see the people I love nourished and happy. But, my husband and kids help with clean up and often take over the task of cooking dinner. I aspire to be like these female saints in my past, but I have recently decided that I need to take care of myself too. Women often deny themselves the same love and outreach that they give freely to others. Self-love is a new journey for me, but one that I'm hoping will be passed down to my own daughter, along with the tradition of selflessness shown by the women in my family. And as for worry...well, some roots just run too deep.

POEM #9

I woke up today to watch the sun set
It's most intense in the moments before it leaves;
in the moments before the hills smother it.
These hills around me, I would trade for nothing
Every evening they take away, but give just the same
Their ebb and flow of celestial allowance keeps life exciting;
It is the reason to wake up.
There are two sides to this valley,
I sit on the side not yet in shadow.
I sit, looking oaks in the eyes.
The trees are like children, left alone in an unfamiliar place,
stretching towards the sun's rays in hopeless desperation,
waiting for day to return.
The sun sinks and my world, for a few moments, is grey.
With the night comes the cold.
and the shadows.
the stars.
moon.
I am like the trees:
If I had only gone further,
the sun may not have left me so soon.

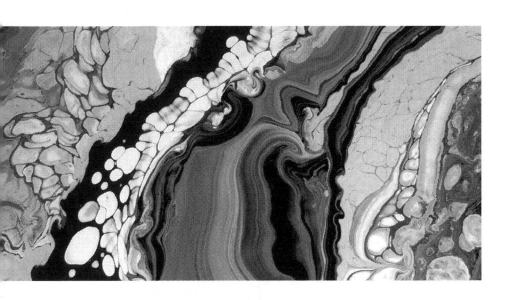

COOL ACRYLIC
Jessica Held

THE HOUSE OF FICTION

In an old church,
now a gathering place for the arts,
one hundred people sat enthralled
as the storyteller spun her tale—
a girl of long ago poised to sin,
hovering at the kitchen door, ready
to run the quick wet yards to the dark barn
where a young man waits in the warm earthy
fragrance of hay. We could hear the night
clicking wild with insects, felt bare toes
touch the first damp blades of grass,
the hard dirt cool on our heels, then…
motion, sirens, the impossible
words: Take cover…
tornado coming!

In the sudden green light, we blinked,
looked around us for the barn, the girl,
undecided what was real, and what was not.
Prompted again to move toward safety, we rose,
walked the unbelieving distance to the door,
some descending obedient to the basement,
some bold and raging into the storm,
eyes and fists raised
to dare the churning sky,
the quaking hills and trees
to strike us down, take back
the untold story,
and return
the house of fiction
to its god.

PROTO

The adventure began long ago
At seven going on forty
Beyond the backyard
And into the forest
Armed with all of nothing
Except a curiosity of a boy
And a knowledge of an age
Amid fallen oaks and elms
And mossed giants
Lain august and majestic
Underneath canopies
Of gnarled limbs and empty nests
Through sentinels of beeches
Still holding on to crispy leaves
Hanging as life does --
On the cusp of spring
Over leaf-littered hills
Around thickly thorned bushes
Emerged a creek whispering
With secrets only meant for him
So he listened and he heard
Within the trickles awaited
Signs of a childhood dream
To uncover a creature
Symbolic of an early time
Beneath the weight of stones
A woken man who sought
Adventure and found it
In a salamander

Andrea Johannes

I REMEMBER YOU

I remember
walking on the bike path
along the river
and looking up to see
a cornflower blue sky
and a white X
where the path
of two jets
had overlapped.

I remember
sitting beneath
a full moon
by the river
the overhanging petals
of a cherry blossom tree
illuminated by warm spotlights
and talking with my classmates
long into the night
long after
the lights had gone out
long after
the moonlight had faded
our voices rising
and falling
like breath
inhaling
and exhaling
like a heartbeat
sounding
in the stillness
an echo
of happiness.

I remember
the edges
of the Hocking River
rising
and falling
with the spring rain
the water spreading
reaching out
towards the town
like liquid fingertips
and then receding again
as if to say,
"I release you,
but I'm still here
running through you
moving
changing
don't forget me."

Athens, Ohio
I remember
you.

SMALL POTS
Jennifer L'Heureux

Jessica Cory

ELEGY FOR THE ORIGINAL BURRITO BUGGY

You bore witness to my bad decisions,
drowning my sorrows deep in burritos.
Post-breakup or post-bender emotions
were negated with taco torpedoes.

Though guac was extra, no one seemed to mind,
Nor the heaping spoonfuls of sour cream.
The only pain, that never-ending line,
Athenians trying to chase their dreams.

Your paint job was a beacon, day or night,
calling the starving and the weary home.
That purple, orange, and yellow beam of light
made us wanderers feel less alone.

The corner of Union and Court Streets bare,
save for the meter maids out on patrol,
creates in my stomach a deep despair,
only your chicken chili can make whole.

Your absence leaves an empty parking space
that other food trucks only dare to fill.
Just know that no one else can take your place;
I know, for me, that no one ever will.

MY GRANDMOTHER ATTENDS THE ATHENS QUILT NATIONAL, 1979

In her world, the fabric recovers what it once
clothed, garments stained or worn so thin
that she had to salvage the best with scissors,
then rock the treadle to piece corduroy to wool

to flannel in a starburst that, like a wood fire,
warms three times. Nothing frivolous, nothing
fancy, except for a burial quilt too bleak to abide
that she edged in lace and pearl buttons taken

from the baptismal dress. Under "Do Not Touch,"
she fingers a manatee's taffeta fins, the tessellated cape
of a matador, and finally, a school of Escher fish

that shifts into a skein of geese as the pattern moves
from sea to sky. "You know they've done what they can,"
she finally says, "but these quilts are nothing but art."

THE THREE POEMS I DIDN'T WRITE

I didn't write three poems this morning.
I got about halfway through each
and stopped. So this is my last try,
but to be honest, it doesn't seem
to be going much better.

The first was a poem about searching,
but I couldn't decide what it was searching for,
a specific image, maybe, or a decent line
that proved too elusive. In the end,
I don't think it was searching for anything,
rain falling on a winter morning,
the smell of coffee.

I never did figure it out, so I wrote
a few lines about the blue jays
wintering on the hillside
behind the house, their bright tufts
glistening among the grey branch
of a stump they poke and prod each morning,
peeling back layers of wet bark
in search of their own lost causes.

You stupid birds, I thought,
but what do I know?
They keep coming back.
I hear the shriek of their approach
as they cruise the underbrush,
searching for something they cannot find
before falling back into the trees,
the silence after they're gone.

A POEM ABOUT ATHENS

The prophet says:
"Town, small city, biograph,
people on the plain near the river,
rain tells its story of blind purpose;
the wind will blow."

We say:
"As town and people,
we are the family names of places we belong
and we are strong.
Make us good citizens,
even when eyes are dulled and dreamy and we forget."

Tonight:
red singe of sundown, fleeing,
lamp-lit shop for leather, flowers,
bells, and buddhas,
brickwork streets, the pacific, open, college green
seized in place at the bell tower.

Here:
good Athenians, we examine our lives.
We commend our prophets and our profs.
We do everything, in Athens.

We write and read and sing.
We cry and spread our hands wide to beg.
We confess and with our eyes we love out loud.

On the Hocking:
river trees tug at the world.
Their living greed for life
knots and fidgets underground.
They look like trouble when storms come.
Tonight, they are what the land says.

 I say:
"Democracies of spirit make us all politicians.
Festivals, celebrations, great events,
causeways reach toward where the road urges.
Athenians, everywhere, be yourselves!"

As you can see:
I've started placing pictures in my poems.

Free-spirited, love-loving citizen, mine,
I know what you'll do
next time we meet at Donkey.
Placing an Americano back on the table,
you'll say:"Do what you like, man. It's cool."

CONTRIBUTORS

Maura Kennedy Anaya, raised in the orange dirt of the Ozark mountains, is a recent transplant to Athens, currently procrastinating completion of her second novel. Reading, dreaming about future gardens, and exploring nature with family may keep her from writing but she swears poetry saves her every single day.

John Aylesworth grew up in Cincinnati and has lived in Athens for 40 years. After he earned an M.A. in English/Creative Writing and studied with Stanley Plumly, Paul Nelson and Walter Tevis, he took a year off, then earned a Ph.D. in Comparative Arts. His dissertation was on the subject of American Neoclassicism as it was realized in works by Washington Irving and Horatio Greenough. Since then, he has taught students in Vinton and Athens County who are Learning Disabled – either physically or emotionally or cognitively. He also raised a family and 3 dogs over the last 30 years.

Ivars Balkits' poetry and prose has been published in numerous literary online and print publications and anthologies. He is a recipient of two Individual Excellence Awards from the Ohio Arts Council, for poetry in 1999 and creative nonfiction in 2014. His one-act play *Spirit Band of Mount Nebo* was selected for the 2013 Hodge Podge Reading Series at Arts/West in Athens, Ohio

Todd Bastin has lived in Athens since 1968 when his parents moved here and he was an infant. He resides in town just below the peak of North Hill with his wife Alyssa, who teaches philosophy at the university. He works at Athens Public Library, where he organizes programs for adults and brings in art shows. He is a life-long writer of poetry, short stories and plays. He hopes that the hills of the Hocking Valley will always be wooded and its waters always clean to drink.

Megan Bee writes with an unquenchable wanderlust and a raw love for the land. Her music is a blend of distinctly homespun vocals, acoustic simplicity, and winsome storytelling. Her album *Like a Canyon* received The Ohio Music Awards Best Americana and Best Singer-Songwriter Album, and won her a finalist spot in the 2018 USA Songwriting Competition. She bases out of the rolling hills of Athens, Ohio and frequently roams the country playing festivals, coffeehouses, brewpubs, house concerts, and campfires.

Alyssa R. Bernstein has taught philosophy at Ohio University since 2002. She lived in New York State through college (except for a wonderful high school year in Finland), then mainly Massachusetts. She came to Athens for a job interview and got charmed. Later she met her husband, a native, at its public library. He loves Athens and vividly remembers its different historical stages, so that now Alyssa, too, seemingly remembers them. She is grateful to Patricia Black's Evening Poets group.

Margaret Black is a quiltmaker residing in rural western Pennsylvania. She enjoys the rhythm and repetition of cutting fabric and sewing it back together. She works mostly in solid cotton fabric, some hand dyed. She relies on color and value placement and the cut, lines, and shapes to create the abstract patterning of her work.

Patricia L.H. Black grew up with a father who loved poetry and quoted it so much she never had a chance. She has lived in Athens for most of her adult life, working under a variety of hats – Ohio University editor, travel agent, librarian/bookmobile driver, secretary and general dog's-body back at Ohio University. She discovered she was born to retire. She is involved in the Athens Poetry Group, the PentaPoets, the Evening Poets and the Ohio Poetry Association.

Trevor Bratton is a Geological Sciences student at Ohio University, from Lancaster, OH. He began his path at OU in 2008, pausing in 2010. He continued to live in Athens until 2012, when he moved to Columbus. Trevor took up residence in Nelsonville and returned to his studies in 2018, drawn back by the peacefulness and closeness to nature afforded by living in Athens County. While not the focus of his studies, language and its expression has always been an essential part of Trevor's life.

Illustrating since he was in grade school, **Joe Brumfield** went on to become an editorial cartoonist for his high school newspaper, then on to Marshall University's Parthenon. He won numerous first place Associated Press awards for his work in southeastern Ohio's Athens Messenger. Serving as the Cannabis Museum's Curator over the last 6 years led him into a trove of art, images and artifacts that date back more than 200 years, which has been extremely influential to his most recent works.

Jared A. Butcher, Jr. is a local writer who would prefer to remain anonymous but has agreed to reveal himself for the sake of W.W. Fardels Bear who came into existence on the 6th of June, 1996, while he was serving as the "potter's assistant" to his (real life) daughter. Fardels, is the inspiration for all that is humorous in Butcher's writings. His collected works were published almost exactly 19 years later in *Blue Prints,* and read by his daughter at the "Author and Illustrator Fair" held at the Athens Public Library in 2015

Devin Aeh Canary was born and raised in Nelsonville. She was awarded the ACLU's Courageous Advocate Award while in high school for creating and distributing an underground paper despite the administration's threats to expel her. She is a homeschooling mama of two and co-founder of Canary Acres Animal Sanctuary in Glouster. Devin is a wannabe witch who believes that words, spoken or written, can be magic spells that alter someone's existence, for just a minute or for much longer. She believes poetry is powerful...poetry is witchcraft.

Dan Canterbury is the prodigal son of a Baptist minister. He grew up in a musical family. When he composes, often songs will begin as poems. A song lyric will distill out of the poetry, followed shortly by a melody. His approach to songwriting focuses on the importance of the lyric, allowing the craft of songwriting to remain visible to the listener, through the interplay of syllables, tempo, texture, and tone. As much as he hates to admit it, as it remains the bane of his existence otherwise, he does some of his best writing on his 90+ mile commute from Athens to Columbus.

Kiki Chen: Born in Athens, OH. Lives in Athens, OH. Currently a senior at Athens High School (Class of 2019). Loves, but hoping to someday leave, Athens, OH. Likes: sharks, solitude, & sandwiches. Dislikes: villainization of sharks, loneliness, & the stigma on double-texting — she has a lot to say. This is her first work published in a book.

Jessica Cory is a native of southeastern Ohio now living in western North Carolina. She is the editor of *Mountains Piled upon Mountains: Appalachian Nature Writing in the Anthropocene* (WVU Press 2019). Her creative work and criticism is forthcoming or appears in the *North Carolina Literary Review, A Poetry Congeries, Menacing Hedge, ellipsis...,* and other wonderful journals. She teaches in the English Department at Western Carolina University.

Exploring the edges of both painting and photography, **Tim Creamer** has been creating images that have the soul of art coupled with reality of a photographic image. Utilizing mobile devices to both capture and transform, he creates a synthesis of his subjects to transcend surface qualities of a moment or scene.

Raised in Athens County, **Bruce Dalzell** moved away many times to the bright lights of somewhere else. But he always returned to attempt a life in a small town. Husband, father of three, songwriter, piano tuner, he has 5 albums of original songs, three of music written for film, appeared on NPR's Mountain Stage. He produced and engineered two albums of songs written by Passioworks artists and local musicians. Being a grandfather is his latest and most consuming effort.

Robert DeMott's poetry books include *News of Loss* (Bottom Dog Press, 1994), *The Weather in Athens* (Bottom Dog Press, 2001), recipient of the 2002 Ohioana Poetry Award, and *Brief and Glorious Transit: Prose Poems* (Pudding House, 2007). He taught at Ohio University from 1969 to 2013. His recent books are *Astream: American Writers on Fly Fishing* (2012), *Steinbeck's Typewriter: Essays on His Art* (2012), *Angling Days: A Fly Fisher's Journals* (2016), and *Conversations with Jim Harrison*, Revised and Updated (2019).

April Felipe received her B.F.A from The New York State College of Ceramics at Alfred University and her M.F.A in Ceramics from Ohio University. April has set down roots in Albany, Ohio with a home studio. She currently works teaching art through the Dairy Barn Arts Center and Arts West.

Liana Flores is Mexican-american/ Beautiful/ Strong/ Energetic and Caring/ Mother./ She is the Lord's Daughter/ Faithful/ Dedicated/Animated and Loving/ Wife./She is Blue/ Like the Deep/ Mysterious/ Dark Depths/ Of the Sea;/ She is me.

Kate Fox's work has appeared in the *Great River Review, Kenyon Review, New Ohio Review, Pleiades, Valparaiso Review*, and *West Branch*. She is the author of two chapbooks: *The Lazarus Method*, published by Kent State University Press as part of the Wick Poetry Chapbook Series, and *Walking Off the Map*, published by Seven Kitchens Press. Kate earned her Ph.D. in American literature/creative writing from Ohio University and lives in Athens with her partner, Robert DeMott, and their two dogs.

Jane Ann Fuller is a recipient of the James Boatwright III Prize (R.T. Smith). Her poetry appears in *Shenandoah, Atticus Review, Fifth Wednesday, Grist, Sugar House Review, Rise Up Review, Project Hope, All We Know Of Pleasure: Poetic Erotica by Women, The American Journal of Poetry*, and elsewhere.

Felix Gagliano was born in New Orleans in 1938. After receiving his Ph.D. at the University of Illinois, he moved to Athens in 1970. At OU he was Chair of the Political Science Department, Vice Provost for International Programs, and Director of the Center for International Studies. He is devoted to his four children, their spouses and his ten grandchildren. After retirement in 1999, he became a co-founder and active participant in the Athens Library Poetry Group.

Jeffrey Hanson worked as a construction laborer, landscaper, security guard, janitor, journeyman roofer, and U.S. sailor before receiving an MA in American Literature at San Diego State University and a Ph.D. in Creative Writing at Ohio University. He taught writing for thirteen years in southeastern Ohio prisons. He currently teaches as an adjunct Professor for Ohio University. His work has appeared in *The Adroit Journal, Blue Collar Review, 34th Parallel, Forge, Blood Orange, Houston Literary Review,* and *Poetry Pacific*.

Hayley Mitchell Haugen holds a Ph.D. in American Literature from Ohio University and an MFA in poetry from the University of Washington. She is an Associate Professor of English at Ohio University Southern, where she teaches composition, American literature, and creative writing. Her chapbook *What the Grimm Girl Looks Forward To* appears from Finishing Line Press (2016), and her full-length collection *Light & Shadow, Shadow & Light* from Main Street Rag (2018). She edits *Sheila-Na-Gig online*: https://sheilanagigblog.com/ and *Sheila-Na-Gig Editions*.

Jessica Held first moved to Athens, Ohio in 1994 to study painting and photography at Ohio University. After receiving her degree and after several moves, she settled back in Athens. Jessica continues to exhibit her artwork and owns a small business selling her painted functional artwork in shops around Ohio.

Teagan Hughes was born in 2002 in Eugene, Oregon, and moved to Athens in 2006. She began writing poetry and fiction in fourth grade and hasn't stopped since. She also participates in community theatre. She is in the class of 2019 at Athens High School.

Brytton Jarrett (McQuire) is a graduate of Ohio University with a Bachelor of Specialized Studies degree in the Creative Arts. She spent most of her life living in Athens, OH and currently resides in Huntington, WV working as a freelance mixed media artist and musician, along with her husband Brett Jarrett. Brytton was inspired by the haunted history of Athens to create a watercolor collage of The Ridges, one of the well known haunted 'hot spots' in the area.

Meredith S. Jensen is a full-time communication professional and part-time faerie. For employment, she's a librarian for the Athens County Public Libraries and freelance writer, primarily as a contributor to magazines The Sunday in Las Vegas and Mirror in Athens. For enjoyment, she's an artist, gardener, birder, hiker, performer, and all-around adventurer. She lives in the woods of Athens County with her partner, two gremlins, and an umbrella cockatoo.

Andrea Johannes lived in Athens from 2008-2018. She studied Applied Linguistics at Ohio University and later taught English in the Ohio Program of Intensive English. Although Andrea has recently relocated to Philadelphia and now works as an Adjunct Lecturer at the University of Pennsylvania, she continues to be a member of an evening poetry group in Athens. Andrea's favorite memories of Athens are spending time with friends at the Village Bakery and taking walks on the bike path.

Sean Kelbley is a Nelsonville native, raised in southeastern Ohio and Maine, and currently residing near Albany in a house he and his husband built. He is an Athens City Schools K-6 counselor. "True Story," originally published by *The Rise Up Review*, was nominated for Best of the Net 2017. Recent work is at *Crab Creek Review, One, Rattle*, and elsewhere. In 2018, Sean was a poetry contest finalist at *Still: The Journal, Midwest Review*, and *Up North Lit*.

Stephanie Kendrick is an amateur poet living in Albany, Ohio with her husband and son. A graduate of Ohio University, she works as a Service and Support Specialist with the Athens County Board of Developmental Disabilities. She likes cats, Brazilian Jiu-Jitsu and her hammock. She has unhealthy relationships with people-watching and reality television. Her poems have appeared in *Sphere*, Women of Appalachia Project's *Women Speak 10th Anniversary Collection* and *Not Far from Me: Stories of Opioids and Ohio*.

Pamela Kircher's poems have been published in many journals and in *Best American Poetry 1996*. She was granted four Ohio Arts Council Individual Artist Fellowships and a MacDowell Colony fellowship. *Whole Sky*, a full-length collection, was published in 1996. *Light's Shadow*, a chapbook, was published in 2001. She lived in Athens, the town of her forebears, for fourteen years. Her great-grandfather was a contractor who built Ellis Hall, a home on Second Street, and other buildings across the county.

Marlene L'Abbe's artistic emphasis is fueled by inspirations that portray her experience of life and the world of nature. She studied art in Montreal in the early seventies and currently lives in Athens, OH. She markets her art tiles world wide under the name Waterspider Designs. Marlene is author (then, Marlene Rudginsky) of the *Flower Speaks* card and book set (US Games Systems, 1999) and enjoys writing poetry.

Becca J.R. Lachman works in the magical world of public libraries. Editor of *A Ritual to Read Together: Poems in Conversation with William Stafford*. She's also the author of two poetry collections: *Other Acreage*, an ode-elegy to her family's 1840s dairy farm, and *The Apple Speaks*, which explores being a wife/daughter of loved ones doing nonviolent peace work in war-torn places. Recent poems and essays appear in *Connotation Press, Consequence Magazine, Image*, and *So to Speak: A Feminist Journal of Language & Art*.

Leadership Athens County (Athens County Foundation) is a nine-month course aimed at developing a corps of informed citizens to provide dynamic community leadership. Participants explore Athens' economic, political, social and cultural landscape through discussions of current issues and conversations with community leaders. This is a tremendous opportunity for both personal and professional growth. Participants become aware of, examine and learn about the social, economic and environmental needs of the community to develop a common ground for working together on present and future community needs.

Cathy Cultice Lentes first visited Athens when her high school marching band performed during halftime at an O.U. football game. After brief attempts at city living, Cathy moved to Meigs County in 1987, and has been traversing the winding roads back and forth to Athens ever since. A former member of Calliope Feminist Choir and an ongoing participant in the Women of Appalachia Project, Cathy can often be found teaching, reading, or writing at some Athens venue.

Chris Leonard is a near-lifelong resident of Athens county and attended both Federal Hocking High School and Ohio University. He is a member of and mentor for The Athens Photo Project. He is an avid reader, an occasional writer, and an enthusiastic collector of old manual typewriters.

Jennifer L'Heureux is the story of small business in progress. She has continually worked and has been a part of the Athens Art and Small Business Community for decades now. She will call herself a potter, but truly, she is the owner of a really cool, locally eclectic retail shop called the Nelsonville Emporium.

Svenn Lindskold, an English major graduate of Wayne University, served as a draftee in the U. S. Army, worked as a municipal personnel director in Florida, as a professor of social psychology at Ohio University, and as a volunteer environmental activist in Florida. His wife, Joy, an artist and writer, and he self-published annual chapbooks of their poetry from 2011 until her death in 2016.

Eileen Lynch is a retired family law paralegal who specialized in domestic violence. She assisted victims in shelters and a Prosecutor's office. Eileen moved to Athens County in 2011. She loves to write and has been creating stories for forty years. She also designs and sews wearable art and creates hand quilted wall hangings. Eileen believes her greatest accomplishment was rearing her four children who are now all happy, productive adults.

Wanda Lynn Wheeler Mains was born in Mt. Kisco, New York, and began writing poetry in the 1st grade, in Hazleton, Pennsylvania. She took the 7th and 8th grade in one year through a "Speeder's Course" from Penn State, along with 30 other kids. She was associate editor of her high school paper, and won all spelling contests. Wanda was an assistant manager for Avon, and is an Avon representative now. In addition, she is a pianist for the Athens Seventh Day Adventist Church, where she is also a Personal Ministries Leader and Communications Secretary.

Michael McDowell was raised on the east coast just out of New York City. He always loved art but particularly was intuitively good with his father's black and white Polaroid camera. He has done many creative things with his life with various levels of success. He traveled with The Band in the 70s but wound up in Athens about 20 years ago and became involved with Athens Photo Project about 10 years ago.

Wendy McVicker, poet and Ohio Arts Council teaching artist, is the author of the chapbooks *The Dancer's Notes, Sanctuary*, and (with Athens artist John McVicker) *Sliced Dark*. She loves stirring up poetry wherever she can, and collaborating with other writers, artists, dancers, and musicians. Her poems have appeared in various journals and anthologies over the years, most recently *The BOOM Project: Voices of a Generation*. She performs solo or with musician Emily Prince as the duo *another language altogether*.

Jean Voneman Mikhail has resided in the Athens, Ohio area since 1982, except for time she spent teaching in Asia. She has published in *Fifth Wednesday Journal, Pudding, Red Wolf Journal*, and in an anthology entitled *#QUEER*. She believes that writing poetry can transform and even save people's lives because it manages to share the very personal in the safe environment of the page.

Dinty W. Moore is author of the memoir *Between Panic & Desire*, the writing guide *Crafting the Personal Essay*, and numerous other books. He has published essays and stories in *The Georgia Review, Harpers, The New York Times Sunday Magazine, The Southern Review*, and elsewhere. He directs Ohio University's graduate creative writing program, edits *Brevity*, a journal of flash nonfiction, and lives in Athens' Near Eastside, where he grows heirloom tomatoes and edible dandelions.

Shannon Moyer was born in Athens and enjoys the scenery and residents of southeast Ohio. She is an environmental, animal, and human rights activist, and has always enjoyed art of all kinds. She is a member of the Athens Photographic Project and has been taking photos since she was a child.

Melanie Moynan-Smith was born in Montreal, Quebec, Canada and moved to California in the 1970s to work as a nurse. She worked in Idaho and Colorado, and taught nursing at the University of New Mexico. Melanie is passionate about healthcare for all and civil rights, and worked in public health and medical clinics for the uninsured as a nurse practitioner before she retired in 2014. She now lobbies for universal healthcare. She lives in Athens, Ohio with her husband.

Audrey (Deni) Naffziger has published 3 chapbooks, a collection of poems (*Desire to Stay*, Stockport Flats Press) and was commissioned to co-write a historically-based collection of letters and poems (*Revenants: A Story of Many Lives*), which received an Ohio Art Council special projects grant. She served as editor of *Riverwind* literary magazine (Hocking College) for 17 years.

Violeta Orozco is a bilingual poet born in Mexico City. Besides writing in English and in Spanish, she is also a translator and is finishing her Masters in Spanish Literature in

Ohio University, where she has organized several poetry events for the local community and the university. She has won a national poetry award in Mexico in 2014 and enjoys presented her poems in music jams, academic symposiums.

Edith Y. Post writes poems only when something catches her eye or imagination. Many of her poems have been written for celebrations or special events for friends and family. Her inspiration came from her mother whose style of writing was very Dutch. In the Netherlands people are encouraged to write rhyming poetry for birthdays and holidays.

Danette Pratt enjoyed a professional career as a Biological Illustrator and Graphic Artist. Retired, she pursues her personal work in fiber, fabric (dye and embellishment), experimental photography and designing/creating *SeriouslySickSocks* (zombie and classic monster sock monkeys). She resides at her country home and studio located near Athens, Ohio.

Emily Prince works in arts education, professional theater and, as a musician, performs with poet Wendy McVicker in the group *another language altogether.* She is a tireless cheerleader and advocate for southeast Ohio, Appalachian culture, and homegrown artists. When not administrating the arts she is crafting, writing, and spending time on her farm with her husband and sons.

Vicki Pritchard is a Registered Nurse who attended her psychiatry affiliation at the Athens State Mental Hospital in the early 1960s. She later achieved her Bachelor of Science in Nursing degree at Ohio University in Athens, Ohio. Eventually attaining a Master of Science in Public Health Nursing, she has worked in the field of health care all her life, in many types of settings. In semi-retirement, she writes for pleasure.

Bonnie Proudfoot, of Athens, Ohio, has published poetry and short stories, press releases, and movie and book reviews. She is an Associate Professor in the Department of Arts and Sciences, teaching writing at Hocking College. She was a former co-editor of *Riverwind*, Hocking College's award winning literary magazine. Her first novel, *Goshen Road*, is forthcoming from Swallow Press in January of 2020.

Thomas Quinn is an optometrist practicing with Drs. Quinn, Foster & Associates in Athens, Ohio. Born in Zanesville, OH, he attended Zanesville Rosecrans High School, where Sister Deborah, a Catholic nun of the Franciscan order, first kindled his interest in poetry. He has written poetry, with long spells of silence, off and on ever since. He finds poetry, like music, a wonderfully unique form of expression; sometimes stirring, often contemplative.

Betty Ranck is a nature photographer residing in Athens,Ohio. Her images range from expansive landscapes to intimate flora. She participated in the WideOpen International Photography Exhibition at the Dairy Barn Arts Center. Her entry, "Dogwood Evening" was selected to travel to the Sony Gallery in New York City.

R. H. Reilly, came to Athens in 1967 and fell in love with it. After getting her education at OU, raising a family and having a teaching career at Hocking College, she joined a local poetry group and began writing in her retirement. Today, Reilly enjoys writing prose and poetry, painting and volunteering as a CASA/GAL while she enjoys the richness of Athens' life - good friends, yoga, Farmers Market, Athena Cinema and of course, Coolville Hot Club Jazz at Casa Nueva.

Karen Renee is a photographer, musician, philanthropist, and mother of two with a special interest in capturing the human experience. We all have a story to share. This image was captured at the Athens International Street Fair, an event that seeks to celebrate the diversity of our unique town.

James Alan Riley's latest book, *Broken Frequencies: A Book of Poems* was recently released by Shadelandhouse Modern Press. Riley is the recipient of a National Endowment for the Arts Fellowship, two Al Smith Fellowships from the Kentucky Arts Council, and an Individual Artist's Fellowship from the Ohio Arts Council. His work has appeared in a number of literary magazines. He edited *Kentucky Voices: A Collection of Contemporary Kentucky Short Stories* (PC Press, 1999) and was the founding editor of *The Pikeville Review* (1987).

Shei Sanchez fell in love with the power of words as a little girl growing up in Jersey City, New Jersey. A native of Manila, Philippines, Shei immigrated to the United States at the age of seven. Her stories explore life lessons gained from her chronic illness and the contentious questions of belonging. An Athens, Ohio transplant of six years, Shei lives in Stewart with her partner, two adventurous dogs, a spunky cat, and a motley crew of backyard chickens.

Robin Schaffer thinks about rivers, birds on wires, neon lights, dancing and poetry. Her life is focused on helping kids to believe in themselves and their imaginations.

Amy Shaw is a lifelong educator originally from West Virginia, but has called Athens, Ohio home for twenty-two years. She taught English at Athens High School for sixteen years and Writing and Rhetoric courses at Ohio University. She co-coordinated Poetry Out Loud for seven years, and advised the inaugural year of the Women's, Gender, Sexuality Studies chapter of AHS. Presently, Amy is an Assistant Director of Learning Services in the Heritage College of Osteopathic Medicine at Ohio University.

Keegan Shaw is twenty-one years old and is currently a student at Ohio University focusing on creative nonfiction writing, poetry and outdoor recreation. He has lived in Athens, Ohio for his entire life and has a deep love for backcountry backpacking thanks to an early connection to the foothills and mountains of Appalachia. Most of his literary and visual works have been directly linked to the environment and cultures of southeast Ohio, from which he draws most of his inspiration.

Wenda Sheard practiced law and raised three children in Athens from 1979-1998. While away from Athens for 16 years, she earned a Ph.D. focusing on education policy and used her English degree to teach secondary school English in Wisconsin, Connecticut, and China. From 2009-2014, Wenda taught with her husband at an international school in England. She currently lives with a delightful combination of legal, environmental, and educational pursuits, including serving as a Climate Reality Leadership Corps speaker.

Tina Shoup received her BFA at Ohio University, which is located in beautiful Athens, Ohio. She is a graduate student working on a Museum Studies Certificate. She belongs to an artist co-op in Nelsonville, Ohio and manages Majestic Galleries, a contemporary art gallery.

Joseph Shumar is a student at Federal Hocking Middle School. He has lived in or near the woods his whole life. He has always liked dogs. He loves the woods that he has grown up in and around. He has always lived in the countryside. He feels most at peace when he's in the woods. He likes the songs that the birds sing and finds comfort and peace there.

Lee Spellman is a transgender, non-binary writer living in Athens, Ohio. They are currently completing an MA in poetry at Ohio University, where they serve as the

Assistant Poetry Editor for *New Ohio Review*, as well as an associate editor for *Quarter After Eight*. Lee has published one chapbook, *Within, Without*; their poetry has appeared in *Fangle* magazine.

John Thorndike grew up in Connecticut, spent two years in the Peace Corps in El Salvador, married Clarisa Rubio and moved to a backcountry farm in Chile. Returning to the U.S. with his son in 1974, he settled in Athens, Ohio. For ten years his day job was farming. Then it was construction, but always he wrote. A memoir, *The Last of His Mind*, was published by Ohio University Press, and his latest novel is *A Hundred Fires in Cuba*.

Pittsburgh native **Brett Trottier** is a transfer student from Allegheny College finishing up his second and final year at Ohio University. Brett could not be happier with his move to Athens in 2017. The people, the culture, and the music especially have given him a sense of home and belonging. His goal in music is to genuinely reflect aspects of life such as love, joy, sorrow, and peace for those that may forget these aspects at times.

David Van Shoor is a collage artists living in rural Athens County with a wife, two old dogs and a cat. His collages are created using paper, pictures, paint, ink and glue. The viewer decides what it all means.

Grace Brophy Volker is a former Special Educator, actor and playwright from Columbus, Ohio. She and her husband moved to Athens County three years ago after living and working in New York City. They reside in an 1850's-era log cabin, high on a ridge, where he is obsessed with the deer and wild turkeys and she is obsessed with words. She is honored to have her voice included in this worthy project!

Emily Votaw is a journalist, but she likes to think of herself as a writer. The greatest advice anyone ever gave her was to pursue a career she could be passionate about, which is what her mother told her from a very young age. Votaw is also a music geek, and you might hear her DJ some Saturday mornings on WOUB AM. She lives in Athens with her husband and their two sassy bulldogs and her very old turtle.

Michael Walker is a professional painter and teacher working in Athens, Ohio for over 23 years. Michael has also worked extensively as a production assistant to many of Athens' artists and craftspeople, creating works in various media. His paintings are primarily observational, but he often takes an abstract approach to his work, using his experience as a craftsman of ceramics, glassblowing, and woodworking to guide new approaches to paint. You can see more of Michael's paintings at michaelwalkerarts.com.

A freelance artist based in Athens, Ohio, **Keith Wilde** is best know for his murals about town. His artistic interests also include book illustration. He is happy to chat with passersby or connect with people at keithwilde.com.

Erika Williams grew up in Athens and is currently living in Richmond, VA. She teaches at a private preschool and reads, writes, and embroiders in her spare time. Her favorite things include cheese, champagne, the TV show *Mad Men*, getting small, unnecessary tattoos, and when all 15 of her students nap at the same time.

Jackson Williams is a senior at Ohio University studying to be a science teacher. He spends his free times reading fantasy novels, playing dungeons and dragons, board games, and video games, and leading Young Life. He credits his mother for his love of reading and writing and hopes to someday write a novel.

Kristine Williams lives and writes in Athens, OH. She has been both a contributor to and a juror for the Women of Appalachia Project's *Women Speak* since its beginning in 2009. She is currently the managing editor of *Women Speak: Volume 4 and 10th Anniversary Special Collection.* She is the past managing editor of *Riverwind,* a literary magazine out of Hocking College, in Nelsonville, OH. She has been published in *The Huffington Post* and in *Hawk and Whippoorwill.*

Singer-songwriter **Steve Zarate** writes uplifting songs full of medicinal properties. Performing his vast repertoire at many Athens-area events and venues professionally since 2006, Steve is known as a talented, engaging and exciting entertainer. A self-taught guitarist from Columbus, Steve grew to love southeast Ohio while earning three OU degrees before producing his debut CD, *Homecoming,* in 1995 while living in Juneau, Alaska. Since returning to Ohio in 1997 he's released five more CDs, including 2018's *Patchwork of Light.*

EDITOR'S BIOGRAPHY

Three times a Pushcart Prize nominee, Kari Gunter-Seymour's poetry appears in many fine anthologies and journals including, *Rattle, Crab Orchard Review, Main Street Rag, The American Journal of Poetry, CALYX, Still: The Journal, The LA Times* and on her website (www.karigunterseymourpoet.com). Her chapbook, *Serving,* (Crisis Chronicles Press 2018), was nominated for an Ohioana Award. Her poem "The Weeds in This Garden" was selected by New York Women in Film and the Visible Poetry Project to be visually interpreted in film. She is a third generation Athens countian.

Her award winning photography has been published in *The Sun, Light Journal, Looking at Appalachia, Rattle Ekphrastic, Storm Cellar Quarterly, Vine Leaves Journal* and *Appalachian Heritage.*

Kari is the founder and executive director of the "Women of Appalachia Project™," an arts organization (spoken word and fine art) she created to address marginalization of women from the Appalachian region (www.womenofappalachia.com). She holds a B.F.A. in graphic design and an M.A. in commercial photography, is a retired instructor in the E.W. Scripps School of Journalism at Ohio University, a poetry workshop instructor and Poet Laureate, Athens, Ohio.

Made in the USA
Columbia, SC
11 December 2019